The
Power of Lists

Harness the Power of Lists to Think, Plan, and Grow

SYED AKBAR

DEDICATION

To my mother, who showed me the value of putting things in writing so I would never forget what really matters.

To my dad, whose memory continues to guide my steps.

And to my wife and three kids, whose love makes every list in my life meaningful.

CONTENTS:

INTRODUCTION

Distractions, expectations, and deadlines abound in our world. It feels like there are more chores, more demands, and less time every day. We frequently strive to keep everything together while juggling obligations at work, home, and in our personal lives, but we still feel like we're falling behind. The majority of individuals don't fail because they don't attempt, in actuality. Their lack of a system is the reason they fail.

This book is that system.

This book is fundamentally about **lists**, but not just any lists. It involves creating a framework that is personal, practical, and purposeful in order to transform ideas into progress, thoughts into action, and everyday chaos into significant accomplishment. This book will walk you through every stage of organizing your life, increasing your productivity, taking on a big project, or just regaining control over your time and energy.

In **Chapter 1**, we start by setting the groundwork: comprehending **tasks, priorities, and lists**—how they interact and why they are important.

We go into greater detail in **Chapter 2** about what a **task** actually is and how decomposing it makes it feasible.

By reminding you that preparation is key—measure twice, cut once—**Chapter 3** assists you in developing a sound **plan**.

Lists—your personal road map for completing tasks and maintaining focus—are the only emphasis of **Chapter 4**.

Chapter 5 explains how to **execute** your strategy and lists the reasons why, without action, all the preparation in the world is useless.

However, things don't always go as planned in life. **Chapter 6** can help you deal with setbacks and discover practical **solutions** rather than justifications.

Lastly, **Chapter 7** discusses **cleanup and completion**, which includes wrapping up what you began, taking lessons from the process, and acknowledging your accomplishments. This book is really personal, inspirational, and useful. It is based on the idea that the correct methods can transform your life, but only if you accept responsibility, take initiative, and take control of the situation.

Let's begin by writing your first list—because that list might just be the beginning of a better, clearer, more successful version of you.

CHAPTER 1

TASKS, PRIORITIES, AND LISTS

What makes you feel good? What makes you feel sad? What do you want to do? What do you want to get done? What did you want to do when you were a kid? And what do you desire now that you're an adult? What did you want? What is still your goal? Have you given up on some of your old dreams or put them on wait so you can "handle" life?

These questions get to the heart of what it means to be human. They make us face the difference between who we are and who we aspire to be, and between what we're doing and what we want to achieve. A lot of people don't want to answer these questions since the responses can be hard to hear. It's simpler to keep busy with the things we have to do every day than to stop and think about whether we're going in the right direction.

But here's the thing: how can you make your life happier if you don't know what makes you happy? How can you put the tasks that will help you get there in order if you don't know what you want to achieve? How can you be confident that everything you do every day is getting you closer to your dreams instead of further away from them?

What matters to you in life? The famous Dallas Cowboys coach Tom Landry once remarked that the most important things in life are God, family, and football. What matters to you? Is it your family? Is it faith? Is it having more free time or living a more productive life?

Tom Landry's list was easy to read and understand. Three things. That's all. He recognized what was most important to him, and everything else was less important. He could make decisions swiftly and with confidence because of this clarity. When he had to choose between different things that needed his time and energy, he could ask himself, "Does this help God, family, or football?" If not, it probably wasn't worth his time.

Your list could be different. It could be family, work, and health. It could be creativity, adventure, or helping people. It could be financial security, personal progress, and connections that matter. It's not as important what the things are as it is to know what they are.

I really liked the song "Eye of the Tiger" by Survivor. I utilized the song to get myself to go jogging with my pal early in the morning. "Don't lose your grip on the dreams of the past. You must fight just to keep them alive." These sentences encourage you to keep "fighting" so you can reach your goals.

That song helped because it reminded me of something important: you have to work hard to keep your dreams alive. They don't take care of themselves. They go away if you don't actively seek them. Life's daily grind can wear down our highest dreams until they are only memories of what we used to think was achievable.

But here's what I learnt from those early morning runs: keeping dreams alive isn't simply about doing huge, spectacular things. It's about making little, steady decisions. It's about getting up even when you don't want to. It's about getting the work done even when you don't want to. It's important to remember why you started when things get hard.

You may have additional significant things in your life, whether they are on this list or not. You might have a different list, but you should at least have one. You will lose attention or forget if you don't. You will forget about the people and things that are essential to you. This can include your hopes, dreams, and people you care about. Life will make you forget what matters. You can forget things when you're busy, whether you're doing stuff or nothing at all.

The human brain is very good at adjusting to new situations. This ability to adapt is usually a good thing; it lets us deal with tough situations and be happy in a variety of situations. But there's a downside: we can grow so used to being busy or preoccupied that we forget what we wanted our life to be like in the first place.

Take a moment to think about it. When was the last time you sat down and thought about your most significant goals and values? Not the objectives you believe you should have or the ones that sound good to other people, but the ones that really matter to you. Most individuals can't recall the last time they thought about things like this. They're too busy answering emails, going to meetings, running errands, and doing the never-ending list of minor tasks that fill up each day.

People forget things that are important to them. People forget how beautiful their family is while they are preoccupied with work or sports. People don't know how lucky they are to have a wife, husband, parents, children, siblings, or friends in their lives. When was the last time you had a one-on-one conversation with any of them, or as a family? If you did, do you do it often enough? If not, saying you don't have time isn't a good reason.

This forgetting isn't on purpose or cruel. It happens slowly, almost without anyone noticing. You start work a little later so you can finish an essential job. You miss a family meal because you have to meet a deadline. You put off talking to your spouse because you're exhausted. It feels like every choice is sensible and important. But over time, these little compromises add up to a big change in how you spend your time and energy.

The sad thing is that the people and relationships we ignore are frequently the ones that would make us the happiest and give our lives the greatest purpose if we put in the time and effort to care for them. Getting things done at work feels wonderful for a while, but it doesn't give you the deep, enduring happiness that comes from having strong relationships and meaningful connections with other people.

You did one excellent thing already: you picked up this book. If you don't have enough time, that's okay. We'll learn how to make time for the people you care about, among other things.

It's strange that the phrase "make time" is used because time can't really be made. Every day, we all get the same twenty-four hours. We can select how to use those hours more wisely. We may get rid of things that don't help us reach our goals and make sure we have time for the things that do.

You need to be clear about what worth your time before you can make better choices about how to spend it. That's when it becomes really important to figure out what your priorities are. If you don't know what your top priorities are, you'll always feel busy but never like you're getting anywhere on the things that matter most.

Writing down what matters to you will help you remember what's important in your life. But first, you need to know yourself. What do you want to do with your life? You need to know what's important and write it down. Write down your plan and your aim. You need to know where you're heading. You won't get there if you don't know where you're going or where you want to go. Moving backward is the same as staying in one spot. If you aren't making progress or changing all the time, the world will pass you by, according to any businessperson.

Writing makes everything clear. Thoughts can be hazy and imprecise while they stay in your head. You might think you know what you want, but you haven't really tested if your thoughts are clear and explicit enough to direct action until you try to write them down.

Writing also makes you more committed. Seeing your goals and priorities written down by hand is empowering. It makes things more real and solid. It's easier to forget or overlook something you've merely thought about than something you've written down,

The business analogy fits quite well. In a market where there is a lot of competition, companies that don't come up with new ideas and make things better fall behind. The same idea works in your personal life. If you're not working toward your goals and objectives, you're not simply standing still; you're sliding behind where you could be.

So, the first thing you should do is make a list of the things that matter to you. It is fantastic if you already have it. If you don't have it, you need to learn how to get it. That's why these lists are so crucial. They remind you of things, and they also show you how to attain those things.

Lists can do a lot of things, but these two are the most important. They help you remember what's most important by keeping it in your thoughts. It's easy to forget about long-term ambitions while you're busy with short-term responsibilities. A well-made list helps you remember what's most important.

Lists are like roadmaps that show you how to get from huge, vague goals to little, doable stages. "Be a better parent" is a good aim, but it's not clear enough to act on right away. "Read bedtime stories to my kids three times this week" is a clear goal that you can set on your calendar and follow through on.

That doesn't mean it's simple to get those things. It just means you know what's essential to you: the things you desire, the things you need, the activities you want to do, and how to attain them.

This difference is quite important. Lists don't make hard things easier; they make them feasible, they make them manageable. They provide you a plan and a way to deal with problems that might seem too big or impossible to handle on your own. You can move forward even when the end objective appears far away if you break it down into smaller tasks and put them in a logical order.

The Strength of Motivation

Some people find it easier to do things when they write them down. It doesn't matter to some people; it's all in their heads. But there aren't many of these. Writing things down would help most individuals. They get motivated when they read what they've written. A list also gives you motivation, which is the third thing it does.

Motivation is a strange power. It comes easily and in large amounts at times. Sometimes it seems to be completely gone, no matter how vital the objective or task is. People that rely on remembering everything are usually very self-motivated and have great recollections. Most of us require external tools and processes to help us stay motivated and on track.

Writing out your goals and tasks makes them feel more possible. It could be that writing them down is a little step toward getting them done. Maybe it's because writing them down makes them feel more real and solid. Or maybe it's because making a list of your thoughts helps you find links and options you hadn't thought of previously.

It's incredibly vital to be motivated. Religion is a source of motivation for certain people. Some people acquire it from being poor (they're sick of it), being hungry, needing money, or wanting to relax or have peace of mind. Some people wish to get away from debt or the daily grind. Some people are inspired by seeing other people, and that's fine.

People are different, and so are the things that motivate them. What gives one person energy might not work for another. Some people are driven by the desire to help others, while others are driven by their own success. Some people get motivated by spiritual activities, while others get motivated by competition or trying to be the best.

The most important thing is to figure out what really drives you, not what you think should drive you or what drives other people. You need to be honest with yourself about this. Pay attention to the periods when you feel most alive and involved. What were you up to? What were you thinking? What made you want to move forward?

There's a development in Parker, Texas, not far from where I used to reside in Allen. There are large houses on two to five acres of land. I would drive past that neighborhood whenever I was close by. I wanted to be successful enough to be able to buy a house like that. It would give me energy. It would give me the push I need to do things I wouldn't normally do. There was a photo of a gorgeous house and a really expensive sports vehicle in my closet at one point. I looked at them every day. They pushed me to do better.

A lot of individuals find this kind of visual motivation helpful. As long as you know what they really mean, being motivated by symbols of success isn't superficial or materialistic. The house and car weren't simply things; they stood for financial security, the capacity to take care of your family, and the joy of reaching your goals through hard work.

Looking at those photographs every day helped me get back in touch with my motivation. Those pictures reminded me why the work was worth it on days when it was boring or hard. They helped people stay focused on their long-term goals even when short-term problems may have made them feel like giving up.

I worked from 9 to 5 for a terrific company with great perks. Over the years, I had built up four weeks of vacation. I used to work for WorldCom before Verizon. Every year, we had to let people go. There were only three people left in my group. But I didn't worry about it. I never bothered about things I couldn't change.

This way of thinking about things you can't change is really important for staying motivated and focused. It's not just pointless to worry about things you can't change; it's also counterproductive. It takes away energy that could be utilized for good things and makes you stressed, which makes it harder to make decisions and do well.

The layoffs were a part of doing business. Worrying about them won't stop them or make them less likely to happen. But becoming ready for them by learning new skills, saving money, and keeping a happy attitude could help you get through them if they happen.

My wife and my mom are always worried. My brother does too. I wouldn't even notify my family about the layoffs until they were done. I do my best and then hope for the best. I would sometimes wonder what would happen if I lost my job. I would think about it, but I wouldn't worry. I made it into a reason to do something.

It's crucial to know the difference between thinking and worrying. Thinking is, coming up with ideas, formulating plans, and getting ready for different situations. When you worry, you get the same nervous thoughts again and over that don't lead to any useful action. If you think about the possibility of being laid off, you might update your résumé, start saving money for emergencies, or learn new skills. Thinking about layoffs only makes you more stressed and anxious.

To turn possible problems into motivation, you need to change how you think about them. Instead of perceiving layoffs as scary things, people could see them as reminders to stay alert, keep learning, and be smart with their money. This change turns something that makes you anxious into something that gives you energy to do something good.

You need to figure out what drives you. You have to find your way around your area. You need to locate your "house." You need to locate your "car."

The metaphor of discovering your neighborhood, house, and car is about figuring out what pictures, ambitions, and symbols give you energy. For some people, it may be a car and a house. For other people, it could be a diploma on the wall, a healthy family, a thriving business, or the chance to explore the world.

The most important thing is that your motivational symbols really mean something to you, not merely something you think should motivate you because of what other people think or what society expects. If you get more energy from helping others than from being rich, your motivational images should show service and impact instead of luxury and things.

What Lists Can Do

Lists can help you see things from a new angle. Lists can help you get things done in life and offer you something to look forward to. We will read this book and learn the best ways to make and keep these lists.

One of the best things about making lists is that they give you a new point of view. When you have a lot of things to do, objectives to reach, and duties to take care of, it's hard to see the broader picture or figure out how everything fits together. Writing things down makes it easier to evaluate and prioritize since it generates space.

Lists can give you a sensation of progress and forward motion. Even if the chores are modest, crossing them off means you're making progress. This tangible progress can help you get through days when you feel trapped or overwhelmed. Finishing small chores gives you confidence and sets you up for success when you have to face bigger ones.

Lists are things that need to be done. We'll figure out which jobs are the most vital and which ones aren't. That means we need to make a list of things to do. Some things need to be done immediately, while others can be done later. Some are important but can wait, while others are urgent but not significant. Some can be done in steps. We'll go over all of it.

It's important to understand how tasks and priorities are related in order to manage lists well. Not all duties are the same. Some of them have deadlines that can't be changed. Others make a big difference in your long-term ambitions. Some of them are regular maintenance tasks that keep things running well but don't make big changes.

You can make better choices about how to spend your time and energy if you know the differences between these things. You can put your best effort into the things that will have the biggest effect on your life and aspirations when you know the difference between what's vital and what's just urgent.

Planning

We need to make a plan after we have a list. Planning (theory) and action (implementation) are both very significant. You need both of them. What do they say? "Plan to fail if you don't plan."

It's hard to find the right balance between planning and doing. If you plan too much without doing anything, you'll wind up preparing forever without making any progress. If you do too much without preparation, you end up doing busy labor that doesn't help you reach your goals. The best way to do things is to plan ahead and then follow through.

Planning is more than just determining what to do. You also need to think about when to do it, how to accomplish it most efficiently, and what you'll need. Good planning thinks about problems and comes up with solutions ahead of time. It also makes room for when things don't go as planned.

Make a plan for how to do your work in the best way. If you have things to accomplish on both sides of the city, do the ones on the same side first, even if the one on the other side is more vital. This saves time.

This example shows how to choose between efficiency and importance. Grouping comparable jobs together or organizing them by location can sometimes be more efficient than doing the most critical activity first. This can help you save time and energy.

Good planning takes into account a number of things, such as how important, urgent, efficient, and energy-intensive the task is, as well as what resources are available. The idea is to come up with a series of steps that will get you the most progress with the least amount of wasted time. If you have quick and easy activities to perform initially, this could imply doing less critical ones first to build up momentum for harder work later.

Execution

Then comes execution. You need to stick to your plan, or things will get messy. You won't be able to finish everything.

A lot of people have trouble with execution. Making a plan is one thing; sticking to it is a whole different story. You need discipline, attention, and the capacity to start working even when you don't feel like it to get things done. It also means being able to adapt your plan when things change.

The secret to getting things done is to start with little, doable tasks that build up speed. It's better to finish modest things every time than to keep failing at big ones. When you keep your promises, you gain confidence, which makes it simpler to take on bigger challenges over time.

Challenges

A job can take longer than planned, which could hold up other people. There could be emergencies, like having to pick up the kids, traffic, or other things that get in the way. Be open to change. Execution involves being organized, disciplined, and able to give orders.

Flexibility is important since no plan stays the same when it comes into contact with reality. Things will always happen that you don't expect. Things will take longer than you thought. There will be new things that are more important. Being able to change your strategy while still keeping your most essential goals in mind is an important skill for getting things done.

Organization helps you get things done by making sure you have the tools, information, and resources you need to do them well. Discipline gives you the strength to keep going even when you don't feel like it. Delegation lets you use your own time and energy on things that need your special abilities and attention.

Obstacles, Challenges, and Solutions

What is life without setbacks? These are just challenges that need to be resolved. They make you stronger. The initial difficulty can make you feel bad if you don't face it.

This way of looking at issues changes everything. Instead of seeing issues as things to avoid, they become chances to learn and grow. Every difficulty you face makes you more confident and better able to deal with problems in the future. People who have never had to deal with big problems before sometimes have a harder time when they do because they haven't learned how to be strong and solve problems.

The most important thing is to keep this point of view when things get tough. In hindsight, it's easy to see problems as chances to grow, but it's much tougher to do so when you're under stress, don't know what's going to happen, and are under a lot of strain. It's a useful talent to be able to change how you think about problems as they come up, and it becomes better with experience.

Solutions

We will talk about how to deal with problems. Find solutions. Don't merely point fingers at others. Get it done if you have to, especially for a customer. The customer won't wait long. You can find out who's to blame later. It's not always wrong to blame someone, but it shouldn't be the first thing you do. Find the problem and repair it.

It's practical and beneficial to focus on solutions instead of blaming. In the short term, blaming someone might feel good, but it doesn't help you solve problems or move forward. They do. The best question to ask when you're in trouble isn't "Who's fault is this?" but "What can we do about it?"

This doesn't mean that being responsible isn't vital. You can stop similar problems from happening again by figuring out what went wrong and why. But the time is important. First, deal with the problem at hand. After the crisis is over, you can look back on what happened and figure out how to make things better so it doesn't happen again.

Help each other out. This little sentence has a lot of deep wisdom in it. It's simpler to deal with most problems when you have someone else to help you. diverse people have diverse points of view, abilities, and resources that can make it easier to address challenges. They also give you emotional support that helps you get through tough times.

The idea of aiding each other works both ways. Helping others with their problems helps you create relationships and goodwill that can aid you when you need help. When people help each other out, they all become stronger and more capable.

The Truth About Cleanup

What do I mean by "cleanup"? There's always something left over. Things never really end when you clean up. It is similar to the web. I once saw an ad that proclaimed, "This is the last page. You have reached the end of the internet."

This comparison perfectly shows how chores and obligations never end. Life, like the internet, is always coming up with new duties, difficulties, and chances. The goal isn't to get to a point where everything is done; it is to make systems that can handle the constant flow.

Knowing this truth is freeing because it takes away the need to reach some imaginary level of fulfillment. You can be happy with making steady progress and dealing with whatever comes up instead of feeling annoyed that there's always more to do.

Work never ends, just like the internet never stops. Cleaning up doesn't mean you've done everything you need to do for the rest of your life. It means you take care of what's not done, set a new date for it, and go on. Finding solutions is what cleanup is all about. The first plan might not have worked. Change it. Cleaning up also entails checking your progress and giving yourself a reward. Watch a movie, get a smoothie, or give yourself a nice meal.

When you think about cleanup as a continuing process instead of a final goal, it transforms how you manage your life and get things done. You don't try to get everything done at once. Instead, you focus on what's in front of you, make choices about what to do next, and keep moving forward.

Regular cleaning activities, whether they happen every day, week, or month, can keep tiny problems from turning into big ones. They also provide you a chance to celebrate progress and change your plans based on fresh knowledge or changes in the situation.

Are you getting better? Are you more content?

These questions get to the heart of why managing your lists and being productive are important. The main goal isn't to get more done; it's to make a life that makes you happy and fulfilled. You need to change your systems and ways of doing things if they aren't making you happy and healthy.

You may tell if you're making progress by looking at how many things you've finished, how many goals you've reached, how much better your relationships are, or even just how much more in control of your life you feel. The most important thing is to check often to see if your efforts are getting you closer to your goal and make changes if they aren't.

There's no use in accomplishing anything if you're not happy. If your family isn't pleased, they're not with you. If your buddies aren't happy, they aren't with you. That doesn't mean you have to make yourself unhappy to make them happy. But every once in a while, go the extra mile. They will notice and do the same thing.

This information regarding happiness and relationships is really important. If a productivity method helps you get things done but hurts your relationships or your health, it is not worth it. The idea is to make more time and energy for the things that matter most, not to get so focused on getting things done quickly that you forget why getting things done quickly is important.

You need to keep an eye on and change the balance between taking care of yourself and taking care of others. To be able to help others, you sometimes need to put your own needs first. Sometimes, building relationships and helping others might make you happier and more successful in the long run.

<u>Words You Should Remember</u>

We'll look at a lot of significant words during this process, which I like to call a voyage. Most of them speak for themselves. We'll talk about some of them as we go:

- Time
- Priority
- Lists
- Tasks
- Goals
- Execution
- Solution
- Family
- Friends
- Positivity
- Planning
- Preparation
- Discipline
- Responsibility
- Challenges

These terms describe the key concepts and ideals that promote effective life management. Every one of them needs to be worked on and given attention. They work together to help you get things done, set priorities, and make lists in a way that fits with your bigger goals and values.

Time is the most important resource that everything else relies on. How you spend your time depends on what you think is most important. Lists and tasks give you a way to organize your actions. Goals give you a sense of direction and purpose. Plans become results when they are carried out. Solutions help you get past problems.

Family and friends remind you why being productive is important. It's not only about getting things done; it's also about making time and energy for important connections. Positivity is what makes it possible to keep working hard over time. You can succeed if you plan and prepare. Discipline and responsibility make sure that things get done.

There will always be problems, but they can also be chances to learn and grow. Focusing on this whole framework instead of just strategies and tactics sets the stage for long-term success and happiness.

Keep these phrases in mind as you go about your day. They've made my life better. They can do the same for you. Let's make some time.

The call to "find time" is really an invitation to find yourself—your beliefs, your dreams, your priorities, and your next steps. You can't just find time lying around. You make it by making deliberate decisions about what matters most to you and structuring your life around those objectives.

The journey ahead will teach you useful methods for keeping track of activities and lists, but the most essential thing is to build a life that reflects your beliefs and helps you reach your most important goals. The tools and methods are only ways to get there.

Let's find time.

CHAPTER 2

TASKS

What is a Task?

A task is a piece of work to be done or undertaken. To task someone is to assign them a piece of work.

In project management, a task is an activity that needs to be accomplished within a defined time or by a deadline. A task can be broken down into assignments, which should also have a defined start and end date or a deadline for completion. One or more assignments on a task put the task under execution. Completion of all assignments on a specific task normally renders the task completed. Tasks can be linked together to create dependencies.

In most projects, tasks may suffer from one of two major drawbacks:

Task dependency: This is normal, as most tasks rely on others to get done. However, this can lead to stagnation in a project when many tasks cannot get started unless others are finished.

Unclear understanding of the term "complete": For example, if a task is 90% complete, does this mean that it will take only 1/9 of the time already spent to finish it? Although this is mathematically sound, it is rarely the case in practice.

Tasks are things that need to be done quickly. These are things that you need to do and should be on some kind of schedule. Some things cannot wait. They may be urgent or not. A task could be due now, a month later, or even years later.

For example, you have worked so hard and without a break that you're getting burned out. You may take short vacations, but you've planned a big one next year. A trip to China would mean tasks like renewing your passport, saving money, making hotel reservations, or requesting vacation at work months in advance. Tasks like buying luggage or sundries for the trip could easily come later.

This is where planning and prioritizing come into play. Knowing when to do what is very crucial to any job, and this is called prioritizing.

You need to do a lot of work. Now what?

Write everything down. List all the tasks you can remember.

Sort by:

a. Importance
b. Urgency
c. Ease (how quickly each task can be done)

Choose your plans wisely. Don't just work on anything that comes up. You should know what you can delegate. If you can learn it quickly, even better.

Some important points to consider about tasks:

Tasks should align with your priorities.

Consider if they are Urgent, Important, or Not So Important.

Work is important, and so are Rest and Recreation.

Maintain Positive Energy.

Don't get disappointed or dejected with a lot of work or too many tasks. Remember who you're doing this for (yourself, family, etc.—have pictures in front).

Respect your work.

Energy – Stay Positive – Never Negative.

Connect

Add tasks to connect with people. Talk to your neighbors. Visit a church, masjid, or synagogue. Talk to others and try to understand their perspective. You don't have to agree with them. But by connecting, you'll understand them better, and hopefully, they'll understand you. Maybe you'll become friends. Eventually, this will give you a sense of yourself in the community.

The issue is writing all the tasks that you must do. Write everything you remember. If you don't write everything down, then you might forget tomorrow. What will happen—and it *will* happen—is that you will do the groceries and come back home, and you will say, *"Oh, I forgot bread."* You think you will remember everything, but you won't. You are human; you will forget things. So, write down everything you must do. It doesn't matter if it is important or not, whether you must do it today, later in the month, or five years from now. Even if it is filling gas in the car or recording a program on the DVR, write it down. It is better to write it down and not need it than to not write it down and forget. Writing down tasks will save you time and make you more efficient. Some tasks will be easy, and others could be harder. It might take thirty seconds, or it could take thirty hours.

These lists are not set in stone. Later, we will see that changes will be made. Some tasks will be added, some taken out, some moved up, and some moved down. Some tasks will be merged with others, while others will be separated. The point is, the initial list is fluid. Just keep on writing all the tasks. We will edit them later.

The second thing you must do is sort or categorize the list. Sort it based on importance. Wherever you keep the list—be it on a piece of paper, laptop, or your smartphone—mark them as Urgent, Important, or Not Important.

Mark the tasks the following way:

U – Urgent tasks
I – Important tasks
Leave the rest without any mark.

2/1/2025 To-Do List

Call Susan
Feed the Cat – I
Fill up Suburban – U
Get Medicine for Kids from Pharmacy – U

If there is a task that doesn't have a letter in front of it, then it is neither urgent nor important. Maybe you need to get medicine for the kids in the evening and the pharmacy will be closing in twenty minutes—so this task suddenly becomes urgent.

Another example would be that you must go to the bank, but it will be closing, or your bank rep will be leaving shortly. So this becomes urgent, and you will do this task first instead of calling Susan or filling up the Suburban. It will take priority over everything else.

A good example of an important task is your daughter's or son's soccer game. It is not urgent, but it is very important. You can't miss it for any reason—unless there is a family emergency. I know football fanatics who will not miss Dallas Cowboys games even if there *is* a family emergency. Thanks to smartphones and TVs in hospitals, you can still watch the game even if you must go to the hospital for emergencies.

You need to mark these tasks based on importance. Next, you need to mark them based on how quickly they can be done. Even if some tasks are not urgent or important, you still need to consider the amount of time you expect to spend on them for completion. By marking, I mean that you recognize the time to be spent on each task. You don't have to physically mark them if you have an idea about each task.

Suppose you must go to the bank, and you also must fill up your car. You have enough gas that you can easily go to the bank and come back. But the next time you need to leave, filling up your car will be an urgent task. Suppose you must be someplace in a hurry—then you're in trouble, as you cannot be there on time because you don't have enough gas. You can easily avoid this situation by filling up your car after you are done at the bank. Since it is a task that should take only five to ten minutes, you can leave your home ten minutes earlier and be back before you know it. You can then scratch the "Car fill-up" task from the list, and next time you must leave your home, there's one less task to worry about.

So, the "Car fill-up" task will go on top of the list— it doesn't always need to be urgent to be at the top.

Another good example is that you must change the oil in your car. It might not be urgent, but it is important, and you can easily get it done on your way home from work. A lot of tasks will look different when you execute them.

What does this mean? Let's take the "Oil Change" task for example. On your way back, you stop at the shop for an oil change. You get there, and there is a wait. There are people in front of you, and it will be forty minutes before they even touch your car. So, the task you thought would take fifteen to twenty minutes will now take one hour of your time. That's a forty-five-minute turnaround.

Things don't always turn out the way you thought or the way you planned. Sometimes it will take less time to do certain things, and at other times it will take longer than planned or anticipated. These things tend to take care of themselves in the long run—what goes around comes around. It will even out eventually.

One way around this is to call ahead and reserve your slot for a particular time, so that when you get there, they immediately start working on your car and you are done in fifteen minutes. Or you come back during lunch the next day and try your luck again.

Another example is when you go out for groceries, but you also must buy a gift for a party next week. Since you're already out, why not buy the gift now instead of leaving home another day? So, when you are done with groceries, you can go to the other store, buy the gift, get it off your list, and save time.

You must choose your plans wisely. You don't want to work by yourself all the time. If you can easily delegate your tasks, then do it. This way, tasks will be off your list and save you time. You can ask your spouse to do the task for you. If he or she is driving a car that needs a fill-up, then you can ask your spouse to fill it up on their way home.

Your son or daughter can pitch in and do some tasks for you. They will also feel that they are helping with home chores. It will give them a sense of responsibility. But if they can't do it, then don't push it. If you push it and they do it half-heartedly, then quality might suffer. Or you may think they'll do it, and at the last minute you'll discover that the task wasn't done.

All these tasks that you write down should be in line with your priorities. They should move you forward. You are accomplishing something. Even a small task, like renting a movie, moves you forward. It may seem minor, but watching that movie in your free time gives you relaxation. Relaxation and recreation are good—they give your body and mind the rest they need and help prevent burnout.

But if you're wasting time, then you've crossed the line and are now moving backward. You cannot overindulge. For example, if you go out for groceries and buy something just because it's on sale—but you don't need it—then you're wasting time and resources. This is not about saving money. You must draw a line. That kind of distraction takes you away from accomplishing your real tasks.

We've talked so far about ranking your projects and ranking your tasks. Also rank the effort that each task will take. This gives you an idea of how long it will take to accomplish them. You must stay positive. Don't get bogged down by the number of tasks you need to do. Just start doing them one by one and you'll see the list start to get shorter and shorter. You are accomplishing something. You are moving forward.

It's like a baseball game—you don't always go for home runs. You take a single, then move to second base. Somebody else helps you get to third base or home plate. This is the same as delegating work— someone else helped you finish some of the tasks.

You don't have to finish everything in one trip or one day. You must break the tasks down. Some tasks must be done today, others the next day. And some tasks cannot be done yet because they are waiting on other things to be completed first.

For example, you're planning a trip to Australia next year. There are other things you need to do before you can even attempt that task. You probably need to renew your passport, and that needs to be done as soon as possible. Even renewing your passport has smaller tasks that need to be done first. You must take a photo, but maybe that can wait until next week when you plan to go to the bank. You can download the passport renewal form, fill it out, and have it ready. That's a task that isn't urgent but is easy to complete now. You will also need to buy tickets so you can get a good deal. And you may need to buy clothes, especially as the departure date approaches. You need to anticipate and plan for all of these steps in advance.

Respect your work. Whatever task you do, put your sincere effort into it. Do it to the best of your ability. If not, it will show. Quality—or lack of it—always comes out. In this case, you're doing it for yourself, so do your best for *yourself*. If a task is for someone else—especially if it's job or business-related—then you *don't* have a choice. You must deliver quality work.

If someone else is doing the task for you, make sure you've delegated it to someone qualified. A successful person doesn't have to be good at everything. Often, a successful person surrounds themselves with others who are intelligent, self-motivated, energized, and honest. You've heard the phrase *"measure twice, cut once."* The same rule applies when finding good talent. Spend extra time up front. It pays off in the long run.

---

1. **How do you find good people?**
2. **What to look for in a person?**
3. **Retain good employees – it's more cost-effective**
4. **Respect your employees and coworkers**

---

1.   How do you find good people?

How do you find honest people—those who are dedicated, intelligent, self-motivated, and hardworking? There is no single way. You can find them on job placement websites, or someone can recommend them. Word of mouth is often the best—it comes with a reference.

Wherever you find them, you must make sure they fit your requirements. You should interview them multiple times. You must judge them with the same standards.

Only hire them once you've completed your research and are satisfied that they are the right fit. Reject anyone with a character flaw. People with poor character will, sooner or later, hurt your business. Anyone lazy or dishonest cannot be trusted and should be replaced.

---

2. <u>What to Look for in a Person</u>

Search for someone with good character, positive energy, and a healthy home environment. Look for honesty, hard work, independent thinking, and motivation. Seek out people from different backgrounds, with good habits, and who are trainable. They will learn quickly.

Again, *reject anyone with a character flaw.* Sooner or later, they will hurt your team or your business. Laziness or dishonesty cannot be tolerated.

---

3. <u>Retain Good Employees</u>

It is far more beneficial to retain good employees than to replace them. Pay your current employee more if you have to. If a good employee leaves, you'll spend valuable time and money trying to find a replacement. That process takes away from your focus—whether that's on business growth, operations, or innovation.

You'll also have to train the new hire. And after all that, you may still end up paying them the same— or more—than you would've paid the person who left.

Great! Here's the continued revision and polishing of your section, picking up where we left off—from *Respect your employees* and onward:

---

4. <u>Respect Your Employees</u>

Respect isn't just about being polite. It's about showing genuine appreciation and recognition— including fair compensation.

Here are some principles to follow:

Be fair in your dealings. Treat all employees with integrity and consistency.

Pay employees what they deserve. Don't underpay people who are adding value.

Reward outstanding performance. If someone is going above and beyond—doing more than their job description or working above their pay grade—compensate them accordingly.

Foster a positive environment. Create a workplace where people enjoy coming to work.

Ensure safety. Both physical and emotional safety are essential for productivity and retention.

Give bonuses, organize team outings, and celebrate milestones. Even small tokens of appreciation go a long way.

Listen to feedback and address legitimate complaints immediately. When people feel heard, they feel valued—and they stay.

Multiple Lists

Your personal and professional lives may demand different kinds of lists. A list at home could be very different from one at work. You can create separate lists, or combine everything into one master list. Do what works best for you.

Pro Tip: Combining home and work tasks on one list can help you work more efficiently. For instance, if you're leaving the office and you need to pick up dry cleaning and groceries, you can tackle both personal and professional errands in the same trip. That's smart task management.

Keep Moving Forward

Completing one task at a time is progress. It's easy to feel overwhelmed by a long list—but don't be discouraged. The goal is to *keep moving*. Soon, you'll notice you've completed most of your tasks.

Some days, you may not be able to finish everything. That's okay.

Here's what you can do:

Don't let one unfinished task paralyze your whole list.

Move it to the next day or later in the week—as long as it's not urgent.

Focus on what you *can* do now. Knock out a few easy wins to build momentum.

The Reality of Tasks

The truth is—tasks never end.

Life keeps handing them out. You'll always have something to do. That's just how life works. But the better you manage your tasks, the easier they are to handle. The clearer your lists, the less stress you'll feel.

Remember, the goal is *not* perfection. It's *progress.* Bit by bit, list by list, task by task—you'll move your life forward.

CHAPTER 3

THE PLAN

Planning is really crucial. In fact, it's perhaps the most critical element of the whole process, from making the list to doing the work and cleaning up. If you don't plan well, nothing will work. This basic reality is at the heart of any successful project, whether it's personal, professional, or organizational. Planning turns nebulous goals into clear plans, random ideas into planned actions, and far-off dreams into something that can be done.

To make any real progress, planning has to address three important questions:

What do you wish to do?

When you want to get things done.

How do you want to get there?

All good planning is based on these questions. If you don't have clear answers to each question, even the best efforts will be pointless, wasting time and energy while getting little done.

The Strategic Framework: How to Understand Plans.

Let's have a look at what PLANS are before we move on. Plan means how to get everything done. These tasks could be personal, work-related, religious, or anything else. To get all of these things done, you need to work together.

A plan is just a way to become involved—a methodical way to deal with the different problems and challenges that life throws at you. It works as both a map and a compass, giving you direction while also being flexible enough to handle unexpected situations. Plans recognize that life has many areas that need attention and that each one helps with overall success and happiness. In this case, the word "attack" is quite important. It means having a goal, putting in effort, and being intentional. Plans aren't just pieces of paper that sit around and collect dust. They are active tools that help get things done, organize resources, and get things done. When you plan to attack your chores, you are promising to be involved instead of just hoping that things will happen on their own.

Planning Based on Time: The Time Dimension Plan for the future, which means you can make plans for the next five or ten years. You might also make plans for something that will happen in a year. Then you have plans for the next six months to a year and plans for the next six months to a year. Time is the most democratic resource since everyone gets the same amount of it every day: twenty-four hours. The distinction between individuals who attain their objectives and those who do not is not in the quantity of time available, but in the manner in which that time is organized and employed. Time-based planning understands that different goals need different time frames and that success often depends on being able to coordinate actions across many time frames.

PLANS

Family

10 yr.

5 yr.

1 yr.

6 mo.

3 mo.

1 mo.

This hierarchical structure shows how planning works throughout different time periods. Each level has its own goal and requires a new way of thinking. Plans for a ten-year deal with vision and direction. Five-year plans turn a vision into big goals. One-year plans turn big goals into smaller, doable undertakings. Plans for each month break projects down into particular tasks. Plans could be for your personal life, your profession or business, your studies, or your religion. You can place buying a property in your five-year plan if you're not ready yet. To reach the greater goal, you will need to make smaller plans that are both smaller in size and time frame. If you owe money on credit cards, you might want to pay it off in the first few years, if not sooner. Then, over the next two to three years, save up for the down payment so your mortgage is smaller. A bigger job can contain smaller jobs that you need to prepare to do first.

This example shows how planning works together perfectly. You can't reach the objective of owning a home by yourself; you need to deal with debt, save money, improve your credit, and maybe even raise your income. Each of them is a different planning stream that needs to be coordinated with the others. The beauty of systematic planning is that it shows how all the parts are connected and makes sure that all the parts get the right amount of attention.

<u>Scheduling</u>: The Skill of Time Management Planning can also mean making a schedule. You can make plans to split up the work based on what has to be done. If a task doesn't seem vital to you, don't put it off. You should try to finish it if you can and have the time. You might think that washing windows from the exterior is something you can easily put off until next month or the month after that, but if you have time, you should put it on your agenda for the weekend or the weekend after that and get it done.

Scheduling turns plans from ideas into real promises. It answers the important question of when certain things will happen. Even the best plans are just ideas without a schedule. Plans become real things that affect how people act every day when they are scheduled correctly. The example of cleaning windows shows a key point: the risk of always putting things off. People often put off tasks that don't seem important, which leads to a rising pile of undone business. This list of things to do eventually gets too long and stressful, which makes it harder to get things done in other areas. Finding the right times for all the necessary chores, no matter how important they seem, is what effective scheduling does to stop this from happening.

The Eight-Level System for Dividing Tasks

Do your duties in this order:

1.Things to accomplish the next day

2.Things to do every day for the rest of the week

3.Things to do next week

4.Things to do every week for the rest of the month

5.Things to do next month

6.Things to do every month for the rest of the year

7.Things to do next year

8. Things that need to be done each year for the next five years Once the week is out, you need to re-evaluate your list and take out tasks you may have already done or add the ones you could not complete.

Every level has a particular job to do and needs a different kind of planning. The system makes sure that nothing gets missed while keeping the right amount of focus on what's most important right now.

The daily level needs the most extensive planning and the most specific. These are the tasks that will be done in the next twenty-four hours. They need to be clearly defined, have resources assigned to them, and have time set up for them. The weekly level gives you a sense of the bigger picture while still giving you enough information to plan your day-to-day activities. Monthly planning sets themes and goals that guide what happens each week. Setting big goals for the year gives meaning to the work done each month. Long-term planning gives you a big picture view that makes annual goals worth working toward.

At the end of the week, you should look over your list again and take off chores you may have previously done or add ones you couldn't do. This process of re-evaluation is an important part of good planning. Plans are not fixed texts; they are live systems that must change as things change. Regular reviews make sure that plans are still useful and up to date. It also gives you a chance to learn from your mistakes and make better plans for the future.

Five Important Parts of Good Planning

You need to have the following things in place to plan better. These are the basic needs that must be met before comprehensive planning may start.

To better plan, you need to have the following:

Vision: The Strength of Expectation The ability or act of seeing what will or might happen. In other words, being clear about what you intend to do. Where you wish to go. What you wish to do. Make a plan to get there in ten years, five years, or one year. If you don't know this, everything else is pointless. How will you plan your tasks if you don't know where you need to be? Vision is like the North Star for planning; it's the constant point that shows you where to go when everything else appears unclear. Planning without a clear goal is like doing busy work that makes it seem like you're making progress when you're really just going in circles. Vision answers the most important question about purpose: why are these things worth doing?

Good eyesight works on more than one level at the same time. At the greatest level, it talks about the meaning of life and the most important values. At the intermediate level, it turns purpose into specific areas of life, such as work, family, health, and personal growth. At the operational level, it turns goals for a domain into real, measurable results. Vision is powerful not only because it gives direction, but also because it makes people want to do things. When duties are linked to a strong vision of the future, they become more important and help people keep working hard even when things go tough. Vision turns boring tasks into important steps toward something bigger and better.

Belief

Believe in yourself that you can do this; otherwise, you will fail.

<u>Have a clear goal in mind / Goals / Target / Vision</u>

Where would I like to go? Know where you're going. What do you want to accomplish through the list or on a specific day?

You should know what you want. After talking to the customer, you should know exactly what the customer wants. You must convey that message to the design department. If you are unclear, then you won't be able to provide clear instructions. The result would be a disaster. For anything you are doing, you must know exactly what you want, when you want it, and how you are going to get it.

As far as the list is concerned, you should know how many tasks you must do, by what day you must complete them, and how to get them completed.

Mental Preparation: The Psychological Base
Get your mind ready for what you're going to do. For example, I will either go through the list tomorrow or tidy this room and garage. Mental preparation is the link between making plans and carrying them out. It is setting up the mental circumstances that are needed for action to work. Even the best plans can fail if you don't mentally prepare yourself by getting focused,

motivated, or emotionally ready. The second most crucial thing is getting ready mentally. You need to be fresh and ready to tackle anything. You have to enjoy what you're doing. If you don't like what you plan to do, at least don't hate it. These things add up to something bigger, like getting ready for a vacation, buying a house, or buying a car.

The idea of being "fresh and ready" recognizes that how you feel mentally has a big effect on how well you do. Even simple things might be hard to do when you're tired, stressed, or feeling bad. Mental preparation means controlling these things to make the best conditions for doing anything. How you feel about tasks is very significant. You might not be able to love every activity you have to do, but you can tie each one to a bigger goal that gives it significance and incentive. The most important thing is to always remember how each work helps you reach bigger goals that are very important to you.

The Tactical Foundation: Getting Ready Physically

You have what you need to get your work done. You need to buy paint, a brush, and anything else you need to paint the house. You need to make time to buy all the tools you'll need to paint the house. Check to see that you have all the tools you need to finish your work.

Being physically ready makes sure that all the resources you need are ready when you need them. Finding out that important equipment, resources, or knowledge are missing is the quickest way to stop execution. Physical preparedness stops these problems by finding and making sure that all needs are met ahead of time.

The example of painting a house shows that physical preparation often needs to be planned and done separately. Getting the tools and materials becomes a job in and of itself that must be done before the main job can start. This relationship of dependence must be acknowledged and included in the overall plan.

Physical preparation goes beyond just equipment and materials. It also includes organizing your workplace, making sure the setting is right, and making sure everything is in the right place. The idea is to get rid of any friction or barriers that could make things go wrong.

<u>Planning Time – When / How Much / Who</u>

How long is this going to take? Time the tasks / Responsibility.

You need to know—or at least have an idea—how long each task will take to complete. If it takes a long time, then maybe you should start and finish over the weekend. If it's something that will take longer, then maybe you need to take vacation time to get it done.

Block out time for yourself. Schedule time for your tasks and protect that time. You should not do anything else. Your family should know that you are working on your tasks and should not be disturbed. If they need you, they can schedule time after the period you've blocked off.

Surround Yourself with Positive and Successful People / Find People Who Can Help You

Sometimes you need help with your tasks, job, or business. You need to surround yourself with people who are positive and successful. You don't want people who are lazy, undisciplined, or negative.

Make Time

The Operational Framework for Time Planning

How long is this going to take? Time the responsibilities and tasks. You should know or have a good concept of how long each task will take to do. You might want to start and finish it over the weekend if it takes a long time. If it will take longer, you might need to take a vacation to perform your job.

One of the hardest parts of preparing is figuring out how long things will take. Most individuals regularly overestimate how long projects will take, which makes their calendars too full and causes them to be stressed all the time. To manage your time well, you need to be honest about how hard the tasks are, how fast you can work, and how to prepare for problems that come up.

The idea of using weekends or vacation time for longer projects recognizes that some goals need focused work that can't be done by making small progress every day. When you know what these requirements are, you can plan your time better instead of having false ideas about what you can do in a normal day.

Set Aside Time for Yourself

Set aside time for your tasks and make sure you don't do anything else within that period. You shouldn't do anything else. You shouldn't be bothered while you work on your chores, and your family should know that. They need to make plans with you after this period that you have set out for yourself.

Time blocking is a great way to keep planned tasks safe from other things that need your attention. It means giving planned tasks the same level of respect as key meetings. During blocked time, the only things that get done are planned activities. Other tasks are put off until the right moment. The communication part is very important. Family and coworkers need to know when you can't be reached and why. This means that you need to be upfront about your limits and what you expect. It also takes consistency to keep such boundaries so that other people learn to respect them. Be among people who are positive and successful. You could require support with your work, responsibilities, or business from time to time. You should be among people who are successful and positive. You don't want folks who are lazy, lack discipline, or are always negative. The social environment has a big effect on how well planning works. People that are positive and successful can help you reach your goals by giving you support, advice, and accountability. They also show habits and attitudes that help people succeed. On the other hand, negative, undisciplined people can kill motivation and make failure seem normal. This rule works for both formal relationships (like mentors, coaches, and advisers) and informal ones (like friends, family, and coworkers). The goal is not to leave people behind who are having a hard time, but to make sure that the individuals who have the most power over you help you reach your goals instead of getting in the way.

Making Time: How to Optimize Your Schedule

Change your schedule so that everyone can fit in. Set aside time for the things you need to do. Spend time with your family. Take some time for yourself.

How?

The problem of finding time shows that most individuals feel constantly occupied and stressed. Finding extra time isn't the answer because everyone has the same twenty-four hours. Instead, we need to make better use of the time we already have. This means being honest about how you spend your time right now and making conscious decisions about what is most important. Change the order of your plans. For the whole week, write down what you do every day. Stop spending time or doing activities that aren't helpful. For a day or two, don't watch TV. You can record your shows and watch them on your "day off," which is a planned respite from work, home, and chores. Talk to your family about how to make time for you to get your work done. They could be able to tell you what you shouldn't do since you might be too close to "see" or "think outside the box."

This method includes carefully looking at how time is used and then moving it around in a planned way. The first stage is awareness—understanding where time now goes. A lot of individuals are shocked to learn how much time they waste on things that don't matter. The second stage is to get rid of things that don't help you reach your main goals. The next stage is to reallocate your time by focusing on your planned priorities.

It's also helpful to urge that family members be included in this analysis. Because we are used to them, we often miss patterns and habits that other people observe. They can give you honest criticism on how you're using your time and propose other ways to do things that you might not have thought of from your own point of view.

Five-Minute Investment: Daily Planning

Spend five minutes in the morning planning the remainder of your day. Get your mind ready for what you're going to do. For example, I'm going to tidy this room and garage tomorrow, or go over the list. Take five minutes to plan out the rest of your day. This will save you a lot of time in the future. You may then make a plan for the remainder of the day by putting the chores in order and figuring out how to do them. You may not be able to do everything at once. You have to perform certain things throughout the day and then rest at night. You might have had to accomplish something last night that wasn't on your schedule, or you might have finished something that was planned for today yesterday; therefore, you need to take that activity out. You will be able to plan the remainder of the day in these five minutes.

The five-minute morning planning session is one of the most powerful things you can do. This short investment of time delivers clarity, focus, and direction for the whole day. It turns days that could be very busy into days that are well-planned and meaningful.

The process includes looking over the planned activities, making changes for new situations, and making a realistic calendar for when they will happen. It also gives you a chance to get your thoughts ready for the day's activities, which helps you get in the appropriate frame of mind. This short planning session stops you from having the usual experience of getting to the end of the day and wondering where the time went and what you really did.

Sustainable Execution: Rewards and Breaks

Plan breaks and give yourself a treat during them, like iced tea. You don't want to continue on for five or six hours straight. You need to take a break every couple hours. You can either make yourself a snack or drink or just take a break for thirty minutes. To be sustainable, you have to understand what people can and can't do and what they need. Working nonstop without breaks makes you less productive, makes more mistakes, and eventually burns you out. Scheduled breaks help you stay focused and energized, and they provide you time to think and change your direction.

The most important thing is to plan breaks instead of automatic. Planned breaks happen at the best moments and include things that really help you get your energy and attention back. Reactive breaks happen at bad moments and might not really help you feel better.

Rewards have several uses in the planning process. They encourage people to finish hard activities, make positive connections with productive behavior, and recognize progress toward bigger goals. The most important thing is to pick rewards that help, not hurt, your overall goals.

Keeping things in perspective: Why fun is important. Enjoy yourself. Finally, have fun. Some of the things you have to do are important, like work or business, but remember who you're doing them for. It's for you, your family, and so on. You won't feel stuck with all these tasks if you look at them this way.

It may seem strange to tell people to have fun when talking about serious planning, but it's an important part of long-term success. Fun is not only a waste of time; it is an important part of what makes people happy and motivated. Planning becomes unsustainable when it turns dark and joyless, no matter how well-organized it is.

The most important thing is to keep in mind why duties are important. When activities are linked to higher goals and ideals, they become more meaningful than just being hard or inconvenient. This relationship changes duty into opportunity and burden into privilege.

The process of achieving something can sometimes be fun. It feels good to finish planned tasks, move closer to goals, and see your vision come true. This satisfaction is its own motivation, and it makes the planning process stronger.

<u>The Joining of Planning Parts</u>

To plan well, all of these parts must be put together into a single system. Vision gives you direction, goals give you something to aim for, belief gives you confidence, and preparation gives you the skills you need. Planning your time gives you structure, social support gives you motivation, and perspective gives you long-term success. When these things operate together in a way that makes them stronger, that's when the magic happens. It's easier to set goals when you have a clear vision. Having specific goals helps you arrange your time better. Getting ready well makes you feel more sure of yourself. Support from others keeps you motivated. Taking regular breaks helps you avoid burnout. Having the right point of view keeps the process fun.

Planning isn't something you do once; it's something you do all the time, and it changes as you learn and things change. Plans that are explicit about what to do but also allow for changes when new information comes in or things change are the best.

The most important thing about any planning system is not how pretty or complicated it is, but how well it helps people get what they want most. This framework gives a complete way to plan that covers all the important parts needed for success. When used consistently and tailored to each person's needs, it becomes a powerful instrument for turning goals into accomplishments and aspirations into real things. Planning is definitely the most crucial part of the process. It is the basis for all success and the structure that all success happens in. If you learn how to plan, you can learn how to make the life you really want to live.

Have Fun

Last, but not least—have fun. Even though some are serious tasks (some concerning your job or business), keep a perspective on who you are doing these tasks for. It is for yourself, your family, etc. If you have that perspective, then you won't feel overwhelmed by all these tasks.

CHAPTER 4

LISTS

What is a List?

Several connected items or names written or printed consecutively, typically one below the other.

Do something right now. Stop reading, make a list of things you need to do and come back and start reading. I will wait.

The Power of Good Energy in Managing Lists There are usually a lot of things to do. Your list is rather long. So what? Don't let it get to you. Split up and take over. Do one thing at a time. It took a long time to build Rome. Do one thing at a time, and before you realize it, you'll have done a lot of things on your list. Stay cheerful and put some good energy into your task.

This good vibe isn't simply fluff to get you going; it's something you need to do. When you have a lot of things to do, it's easy to feel overwhelmed and see the big picture instead of the little things that make it up. But when you look at lists in the proper way, they can be empowering instead of stressful.

A To-do list for this page may look like this:
•Task One

•Task Two

•Task Three

• Task Four

Cross out tasks as you complete them and move on to the next one. Crossing out things you've done gives you a sense of pleasure and motivation. It turns abstract success into real proof of progress by making it look like progress is being made.

Planning the List: Putting Strategic Thinking to Work
Making the list. What does it mean to plan the list? We need to write down what we need to do now and what we need to do later. Some things you have to do are look for a job or buy a property. To get a job, you'll need to update your resume and your

education or talents. Have professionals go over your CV before you send it in. Making a list is very different from planning one. Planning requires thinking strategically, being mindful of time, and knowing how tasks are related to each other. You have to think about how what you do now will affect your ambitions for tomorrow. Not only are you arranging your tasks when you make a list, you're also planning your future.

A full brain dump starts the planning phase. No matter how important or urgent, write down anything that comes to mind. This first capture phase has a number of uses. It clears your mind, makes sure you don't forget anything, and gives you a full image of your goals and responsibilities. You can't start to prioritize until you've gotten everything down.

The Art of Prioritization: Do What Matters Most

You need to do what is most important. This is vital now. You need to know what is vital and what is not, what needs to be done right away, and what can wait a little longer.

One of the most important skills for managing lists well is being able to tell the difference between what is really important and what just feels urgent. Not all duties are the same. Some get you a lot closer to your goals, while others just make you think you're being productive. The skill is in knowing the difference.

Importance and urgency often don't agree with one another. The pressing activity needs to be done right now, yet it might not help with long-term goals. The critical activity may not need to be done right now, but it is a big step toward reaching key goals. To manage lists well, you need to be able to put priority over urgency whenever you can, but you also need to be able to handle urgent needs properly.

Get at least one important thing done: build momentum

You need to know that you can do all of the duties, even though there are too many of them, if you do them one at a time. If you try to do too many things at once, you won't be able to do anything. You will become angry and fail in the end. You start one, finish it, and then move on to the next one. We know that there will be some things you won't be able to do. If you can't finish it, put it off till later. The idea of finishing at least one critical activity every day builds a base for steady advancement. This way of thinking understands that productivity isn't about doing everything flawlessly; it's about keeping things moving ahead. Finishing each key work gives you confidence, boosts your mood, and sets a pattern of success.

The most important thing is to figure out what "completion" means. There are clear ends to some jobs, such as sending an email, finishing a report, or making a call. Some of these are ongoing processes that need different ways to monitor progress. For these, finishing can entail hitting a certain goal or putting in a set amount of time on the task.

<u>The Ten-Minute Rule: Break Tasks into Smaller, More Manageable Tasks</u>

I read about the ten-minute rule somewhere. Make sure that each task can be done in ten minutes by breaking it up. So, when you have a lot of activities that can be done in ten minutes, write them down and start doing them one at a time. Let's imagine you have to compose an essay with a thousand words. If you can write about 100 words in ten minutes, that implies you should be able to write about 600 words in an hour. The full essay should take about 100 minutes.

The ten-minute rule is a strong way to stop putting things off and get things done. Big jobs can feel like too much since they seem like they can't be done. We turn scary projects into doable tasks by breaking them down into ten-minute chunks.

This method works because it fits with how people naturally think. Even when I don't feel like it, ten minutes seems doable. It's lengthy enough to make real progress yet short enough to keep your attention and energy up. The rule also sets up natural breaks so that people can rest and think between parts.

Think about the example of a thousand-word essay. Instead of having to write a whole essay, you only have to write 100 words. This change in how you see things alters everything. The task gets easier to start, and the momentum increases on its own.

Managing dependencies means waiting for one task to finish before starting the next.

That's a world that is perfect. That's how things should go. But we know that this world isn't flawless. Some duties will be done, while some won't. The cause is different. You could have to accomplish a chore at a certain time of day, and if you miss it, you'll have to wait till the next day or later. Sometimes you won't have enough time that day, or the person you were supposed to meet has had to change their plans, or there is a family emergency, or you're delayed in traffic. When managing lists in the real world, you have to deal with the messiness of existence. Things don't always go as planned. Dependencies make things slow down. Plans that were meticulously made can be thrown off by things that happen out of the blue. Lists that plan for and work with these facts are the most useful.

You can always do it tomorrow if you can't finish it now. This earth isn't going anywhere, and neither are you. So, if you can, just move it to the next day. It takes a long time to write a book. I couldn't finish it in a day, a week, or even a month. I wrote what I could during the day, but then I had to do other things that day. I lost my job at Verizon while I was writing this book. I had to seek a new job, which took up a lot of my time every day. I had to balance my tasks to make sure they were done.

This example shows how list management can change over time. Life gets in the way, priorities change, and situations change. The idea is not to make a hard system that breaks under stress, but a flexible framework that changes while still moving forward.

Know Your Limits: Be Honest with Yourself

Knowing your limits implies knowing what you can do and what you can't do and need help with. Also, it signifies that you realize you can't accomplish some things.

Being conscious of yourself is an important part of managing your lists well. Knowing what you can and can't do, as well as what resources you have, helps you plan realistically and delegate tasks correctly. This information stops people from taking on too much work and makes sure that the right people are given the right duties.

First case

Let's deal with the first problem first. How much of a job you can do? You may not be able to accomplish any task. If you have to add a room to your house, you might not be able to do it all by yourself, or you could require help finishing it. If you can't do it, you need to ask for aid, like a builder or a contractor. You can probably complete it, but you might need support to do it over a weekend or in a week. If you have help, you could put up a fence in a week, but it might take longer if you do it alone.

<u>Second Case</u>

If your car breaks down and you don't know how to fix it, you can fall into the second group. You should know that trying to fix the problem yourself could make it worse before you start. It would be best to have a mechanic fix your car.

These instances show how important it is to be honest with yourself. If you try to do things that are too hard for you, you might not get good outcomes, waste time, and spend more money. Knowing your limits doesn't mean you're weak; it means you're smart.

Prepare

You will need to measure how long the fence will be and where the posts will go before you start working on it. This will tell you what kind of poles, panels, screws, and other things you need to acquire. This will help you figure out how much the whole project will cost. This will also tell you what tools and resources you need. This is study and getting ready. You need to set aside a different time for it.

Planning turns good thoughts into plans that can be carried out. It means finding out what has to be done, getting the right tools, and knowing everything that needs to be done. Getting ready ahead of time prevents the annoyance of starting a task only to find that important parts are lacking.

Put them all in one location so you don't have to go collect them later and put the whole process on wait. Time management is also part of preparation. Always, always, always, follow the well-known rule: cut once, measure twice. The more ready you are to plan, the less time and money you will waste.

The saying "measure twice, cut once" is true in many areas of life, not only carpentry. In list management, this is taking the time to figure out what is needed, assemble the right tools, and plan how to get things done. This initial investment pays out at the execution phase.

No Surprises—Keep a Record of Everything
Put everything down on paper. If you have a lot to accomplish, you can forget what you have to do.

The brain is amazing, but it can only hold so much information at once. Trying to remember a lot of tasks, deadlines, and obligations takes up mental energy that could be better employed for creative problem-solving and getting things done. Writing things down works like an external memory, which frees up cerebral space for higher-level thought. This idea goes beyond just capturing tasks. Make a note of deadlines, dependencies, resource needs, and any other important information. The idea is to build a complete external system that makes it unnecessary to recall things in your head.

Don't be arrogant; plan realistically.

This happens when you think too highly of yourself. Don't be rude to your work. If you value your work, it will respect you. You can't do everything in a single day. You will need to share everything. If you don't, you can end yourself scheduling a lot of tasks one day and taking a day off the following. If you can't accomplish your tasks, you won't be able to do them the next day because you already have plans for that time. Don't do that.

When you are arrogant about managing lists, you have unrealistic ideas about what can be done in a certain amount of time. This overconfidence makes people overcommit, which causes stress, lowers quality, and, in the end, hurts productivity. To respect your work, you need to give it the time and attention it needs.

To plan realistically, you need to be honest about how much time, energy, and other things you have to do. It means making time for unexpected problems and knowing that quality is often more important than speed.

Make It Personal: Prioritize

Make it about you.

Take this personally if you want to do well. Put in all your effort. You could think I'm being overly serious, but give it some thought. If one of the things you have to do is pay off your debt, fix up your house, or establish a business, it will help you get your finances in order so you can pay for your kid's college fund. But now it's not serious enough. Do all of these things, and you will do well. Do you think the world is against you? Finishing your tasks is the only thing that matters.

When you make list management personal, it goes from being a mechanical task to something that matters to you. When tasks are linked to bigger ideals and long-term goals, they become emotionally important, which keeps people motivated even when things go tough. The most important thing is to know why each work is important and how it helps you reach your bigger goals.

Depending on the situation, priorities can change.

There have been many moments when you were doing one thing and something else came along that made you stop what you were doing and pay attention to the new item. I was in the garage when I found out that one of my kids was sick and had to take him to the hospital. I had to leave everything and take my dad to the hospital because his blood sugar was dangerously low. He spent two weeks in the hospital and then two more weeks in rehab. I was entirely off my routine for a solid month.

Even the best-laid intentions sometimes go wrong in life. You need to be able to change your list when family situations, unanticipated opportunities, or other things come up. The idea is not to make a system that is too rigid and breaks under strain, but a framework that is flexible enough to change while still staying on track.

What do you do? Life happens, that's how it is. You can either be mad at life and blame it, or you can move things around to make time for whatever that comes up. Hit back at life with twice as much force.

This kind of thinking shows that you are strong. Good list managers don't let problems stop their work; instead, they adjust and keep going. They know that problems are just transitory and that working hard over time leads to results.

Most of the time, things aren't as bad. You might learn that your family is coming to stay with you for the weekend. Well, deal with it, go on, and work around it. These are the things that make us see life in a new way. Wake up early to get some work done before your family wakes up. Don't make excuses and don't do anything. That will be the worst thing you can do.

On a brighter note, our number one priority at home is Cowboys football. Everyone knows that. The Cowboys' football game is the most important item that day. We will only miss a Cowboys game if something bad happens.

This example shows how your values and priorities affect how you manage your lists. People have different things that are most important to them, but the rule is the same: know what your priorities are and make your lists in that order.

A hierarchy of values that helps you understand your priorities

---

What is a Priority? Why Prioritize?

Below are some priorities for a lot of people:

- GOD
- Family
- Friends
- Acquaintances
- Peers
- Needy
- Homeless
- Poor
- Older People

When there are disagreements, this hierarchy gives you a way to make decisions. Knowing how you prioritize things might help you decide which jobs need to be done right away and which can wait. It also makes sure that jobs that are urgent but not as vital don't get in the way of things that are more necessary for long-term health and success.

Put Your List First: Make Managing Your List a Top Priority

• Be clear about what you want

• Clarification

• Developing your game plan

• Short Term—Now (less than a month)

• Midterm—A Little Later (one month to twelve months)

• Long Term—In the Future (one year or more)

• Establish an agenda

• Small tasks first – Smaller tasks before

• Timing is Everything

• Time for yourself

• Daily Tasks

• Weekends – Start early in the day

• Knowing what to expect

• Establish a rhythm

• Don't budge; do what you have to do.

• The Art of Waiting

Health: Laying the Groundwork for Good Health

Do you want to work out, run, or walk for four to five hours a week but can't seem to get started? Start slowly, doing one hour a week for a few weeks. Then add an hour and do that for a month. Keep adding an hour a week until you accomplish your goal. Don't let it go down once you get there. Do your best. If something comes up and you miss one or two hours one week, that's fine. But you need to get back on schedule next week.

Health is the most important thing that all other accomplishments depend on. Even the best-organized lists don't mean much if you don't feel good physically and mentally. Adding health-related tasks to your lists makes sure that this important issue gets the attention it needs.

It doesn't matter if you're going somewhere else or just visiting. You can still work out at hotels or if you're staying with someone, you can still run outside and find new ways to work out, even if you only have half of your plan for that week. Half is better than nothing. Get a buddy.

The idea that "half is better than none" means that you don't have to be perfect to make progress. It's more important to be consistent than to be intense. Keeping up the pace during hard times keeps things from going completely off track.

Recreation: How Important It Is to Rest and Refresh

Get a hobby. You may study a language, take a class at the community college or online, or garden. Don't pick up a pastime just because someone told you to. Find something you like and do it.

Recreation is not a luxury; it is necessary for long-term productivity. It gives your mind a break, your emotions a boost, and often generates creativity that helps you do better in other areas. Putting fun things on your lists makes sure they get the attention they need instead of always being put off.

Learn a language. Maybe one that could benefit you at work or just for fun. You can learn it even if you don't need it for work to get a new point of view. It will open up new possibilities. You will learn about a new culture, talk to a lot of people, and make new friends.

Learning is a kind of fun that also makes you better at things. It meets the human desire for growth and may also have useful effects. The most important thing is to choose things that you really enjoy instead of ones you think you should do.

Having fun is key. No matter how creative, hardworking, or enthusiastic you are about your job, there will come a point when you will get burned out. It is true, especially if you are working on a project for a long time or doing tasks for a long time without a break, even if you take short pauses.

Even the most dedicated people can get burned out. Recreation is a way to keep your energy and excitement up throughout time. It's an investment in long-term productivity, not a way to get in the way of it.

If you don't have some form of fun or time off. There will come a time when you don't want to go on, and you'll strike a wall. You won't know how to make it bigger. From there, you won't know how to do anything. You won't be able to think of new things. You will hit a wall.

This graphic explanation shows what really happens when you don't take care of your recreation. The brick wall is a symbol of not only tiredness but also a loss of perspective and inventiveness that makes it hard to solve problems.

Being Outside: Nature's Way of Healing

Being outside is a terrific way to relax. Being outside will help you relax and soothe your worries. That's wonderful if you like to hike and backpack. Grab your bag and go outside to hike for a couple hours a week, or maybe even more.

Nature has special healing effects that indoor activities can't match. Studies have shown time and time again that spending time outside lowers stress, lifts your mood, and improves your brain performance. By including outside activities on your lists, you may be sure to get these benefits.

If you live near Colorado, go there. If you live in the east or west, go to regions with wonderful mountains, valleys, or forests where you may hike. Take a break beside the lake. This is really crucial since you can't add to your bucket and do other things at the same time if your mind is already full with difficulties and issues. It will be really challenging.

The metaphor of the mind as a bucket that can fill up is really fitting. Stress and problems take up a lot of mental space, leaving little opportunity for innovative thinking or solving problems well. Spending time outside helps empty the bucket, making room for new ideas and energy.

Weekends are there for a reason. People work hard during the week, but on the weekends they relax. For a while now, we've been doing that. You need to take some time off for yourself and your family. Your family might need to spend some time with you. You should talk to them, spend time with them, and go on vacation with them.

The cycle of labor and rest is a basic need for all people. Weekends and vacations are not just things that people do; they are also important parts of a healthy lifestyle. They provide people time to create relationships, replenish themselves, and keep their perspective.

So, I just put family here. Friends and family are both vital. It's crucial to connect with people in a nice way. So, keep this in mind. It's great to do things like this to relax so that when you get back to work, you're ready to go. You are the only thing that can stop you from moving forward. You will feel better. You will have more energy to keep going. Get the things done that you need to do. You should perform the work you have to do. You will feel good about yourself. Your family will be happy for you. Your pals will be happy for you.

This conclusion brings together all the parts of good list management. Recreation, relationships, and rest are not separate from productivity; they are important parts of it. They provide you the energy, perspective, and drive you need to take on tough tasks and reach important goals.

When you know how to use them correctly, lists become much more than just ways to keep things organized. They serve as blueprints for living purposefully, systematically reaching objectives, and preserving equilibrium in an ever more intricate world. The idea is to see them not as hard rules, but as helpful suggestions that can help you get from where you are to where you want to be.

CHAPTER 5

EXECUTE

Execute

Execute means to carry out and put into effect the plan you have. As far as we are concerned, planning, scheduling, and creating lists do not matter much if you are not able to execute. Execute the plan. Execute the list. You have the list for a reason, and that reason is to finish the job. A very important part of execution is that you must *execute*—you must now spring into action, you must *do* it. And when you are doing it, nothing else matters.

You have time for this task to be executed, and you also have time for other things in your life. If you have time allotted for the tasks, then your full concentration should be on executing the tasks. So, this is the most important thing you must do, and this is where respect for your work comes out.

Respect – Your Work

Respect your work, and it will respect you. We have talked about this before—this is an important task, and you must finish your task. Not half-finish it, not quarter-finish it, not 99% finish it. Finish it 100%.

Of course, there will be times when you won't be able to finish a task or any of the tasks on your list for the day. If it is out of your control, then reschedule them and move on. Otherwise, finish them as much as possible.

Behavior

You must have a positive frame of mind. If you don't have it, then you won't be able to achieve anything. You must be immersed in it. If you don't like doing a task, you will feel miserable until it is finished.

You must *like* doing the tasks. Even if you don't like doing a task or a bunch of tasks, pretend that you like them. It has worked wonders for me—it can do the same for you.

If I don't like something that I must do, I pretend in my heart that I like it, and I don't have such a bad time doing it. For example, I once had to write an essay while doing my bachelor's at the University of Houston. It was a very boring assignment on a topic that I was not fond of. Since I could not put that as an excuse for not doing it, I pretended to myself that I liked doing it. This way, I was able to concentrate more and finish it way before the due date.

If you must do something that you don't like or simply despise, then you can try this trick. If nothing else, you won't feel bad doing it, and who knows—you might even *enjoy* it.

Preparation

What does preparation mean? It means allotting time, resources, manpower, and/or finances to projects you have to accomplish. If you are prepared, then these tasks should go very fast. It should be a breeze doing these tasks.

Do Not Procrastinate

Sometimes you don't want to do anything. You want to watch a movie, go out for a walk, just lie in bed, or chill out. If you have been working continuously for many hours or days, then it might be understandable. Otherwise, avoid this situation.

Understand that you cannot afford to do this. Look at the big picture—when you finish these tasks, you will have free time. Then you will be able to enjoy that time much more, knowing you've completed your tasks for the day, your project at work, or your to-dos at home.

Now you can watch a movie or enjoy time with your family. Suppose you complete a task for a project that is vital for your business. By completing this task, you've brought yourself a lot closer to finishing the project, and hopefully, your customer will sign a contract with you for future projects.

By completing this task, you will feel great, and it will motivate you to keep completing the rest of the tasks one by one.

Keep Checking Your Progress

Tasks

1.

2. Project: *Design Sprinkler System for Mr. Kimbal*

3.

4.

Tasks for Project: Design Sprinkler System for Mr. Kimbal
a.Visit customer
b. Take measurements fo the front yark and the backyard
c.Sign the contract
d.Schedule work

We are talking about two kinds of progress here.

One is where you are going through the tasks, crossing them out, and moving along as you complete them.

The second type of progress is for a particular project. You have a project that you've broken into tasks and spread out over a few weeks or months. You keep completing one task at a time for this project when it becomes due.

Here, too, you must be honest and respect your work so your tasks for the project get completed. Otherwise, your project will be delayed.

For example, one of the projects you are doing has different tasks. One of the tasks is to call the customer to get input on the design and then send the specifications to the design group, and then to the implementation group for the completion of the product. These are three tasks.

The first one is due today. You talk to the customer, but you cannot contact the design group for whatever reason. You move on to the next task on your list while constantly trying to contact the design group. It could be the next day when you're finally able to reach them. Once you provide them with the specifications, you scratch out the task.

Now, a new task will be on your list: to get the completed design back from the design group in a few days to move the project forward. You should constantly keep checking progress with the design group. If they are not ready, then you will have to push them to get the work completed. For this, you might even have to contact their supervisors.

Cut to the Chase

Most of the time, you won't have time to fool around or waste time. Get to the point, do your job, and move along.

Sometimes, at work, people will stop at your cube just to chat. If you have some hot items on your list, then you cannot afford to waste time. Excuse yourself politely and continue your work.

Similarly, meetings can go off-topic if not properly managed. If the project manager is conducting one and tasks are being discussed that are not as important as others, then ask them to concentrate on the issues that need an immediate response.

So, cut to the chase. From our previous example, get in touch with the design group: "Hey, Mike, how are you? I just talked with the customer, and he wants to design the project in a certain way. I have already sent you the specifications in an email. When do you think you can provide a completed design?" Short and sweet. Hold on to the chat for next time.

Positive Energy

Keep that positive energy. Even if something goes wrong, keep that energy. Things always go wrong. Even if it's your fault, stay positive and stay focused.

If it's not your fault, make sure the issue is acknowledged—without pointing fingers. If you have people working for you, then you must keep their morale high.

Quality of work goes down with negative energy. People start to blame each other when bad things happen. If not controlled, this might take down the whole group, company, or even country.

Below are a few points to keep a positive attitude:

Accept who you are. List your good qualities. If you find new good qualities, add them to the list accordingly.

What's done is done. The past is gone. If you did anything negative, learn from it and make yourself better. Start again today.

Forgive and forget. You might not choose to forget, and that's fine too. You can learn from it. Let go of any resentments. Don't look for reasons to blame others.

As they say, time is money. Use your time wisely— don't waste it. Use it to better yourself and others. Don't focus on the negative. Negativity spreads despair and drains energy.

Don't share your bad experiences with others. Focus on positive things.

List everything you are grateful for—your health, your family, your friends, your wealth.

You can heal yourself. Life will give you problems and stress. Leave situations that give you problems. If you cannot leave, then manage the situation to reduce the problems.

Be happy—for yourself and for others. When you are happy, others around you will be happy too. It's not your concern if others don't follow this principle. Do it for yourself and for your friends and family.

Know Your Strengths and Do What You Are Good At

If you are weak in something, educate yourself and make yourself better. Otherwise, find someone else to do it. That way, it will be done better.

Hire well-qualified people.

Build Trust

Building trust goes both ways. You should trust your employees/employers, and they should be able to trust you as well.

Sometimes this is hard. But if you work hard and do good work, it becomes easier for others to trust you.

As for trusting them—make sure that when you talk to your boss or employees, you convey clear and concise messages. No ambiguity. Written communication helps—then everyone can refer back to it later if there's a problem.

If everyone knows what is expected of them, there will be fewer issues in the future.

Find Your Strength

Find what you are good at and then use that in your life to make yourself a better person. Nobody is good at everything. Everyone has strengths and weaknesses. You should not only find your strengths but also accept your weaknesses. This will make you stronger and less susceptible to failure.

All professional sports organizations go through a season and then evaluate where they need help to get better. In free agency, or the next draft, they address those areas to improve their team.

You do what your strength dictates you to do. If you're strong in organizing, then that's what you do—organize. If you are stronger with numbers, then accounting is probably good for you. Or if you are strong in motivation, then motivate people.

You could have multiple strengths or weaknesses. As far as weaknesses are concerned, let others handle them. For things you are not good at, hire people who are good in those areas and make them work for you. You supervise but let those who are good at these tasks handle them. You learn from them—not to replace them, but because by learning, you will have a better understanding of how to do things you're not good at.

If someone leaves, you will have to do what they were doing until you find a replacement. On the same note, don't let a good employee or a leader leave. It will save you in the long run.

Take the example of LeBron James. When LeBron left the Cleveland Cavaliers for the first time, they started losing again and never recovered. It is better to invest in your employee now than to find another one later.

Every Moment Matters

Something might happen that could throw you off course. You will have to reprioritize on the go. Tasks don't change—the priority might change.

Stay on schedule. Say NO if people ask you to do things that can be done later. Say it nicely. Asking them to wait is another form of NO, as is rescheduling for a later time or day. Please make sure you come back to it, though.

It's even better to help them do it themselves. You might spend a few minutes with them, but it could save you many if you did it yourself.

Importance Trumps Urgency in Some Cases

For example, a task that is time-sensitive—like going to a city office that closes at 5 PM—can wait till the next day if you don't have enough time to drive there.

In its place, bump up another task, like doing laundry, or pulling one up from the next day. You might even move all tasks that require you to leave home to the next day and coordinate them with the City Office task so you do them all in one trip.

Are You Moving Forward?

Sometimes you are just spinning your wheels and not getting anywhere. If you are staying still or moving backward, then you are not moving forward. You need to step back, evaluate, and see what you are doing that is making you stay in one place or move in reverse.

Complete at Least One Task to Completion

Before you move along, make sure you complete the task. If it is out of your power, then it's okay to move to the next task as long as you will be coming back to it.

Sometimes it will take longer than you had anticipated, and that is fine too. Some tasks will finish quicker—so in the long run, it will even out.

The importance of finishing tasks is that you will feel good that you are moving forward and that you are achieving something. You will feel successful.

You Should Be Adaptable

Suppose you must buy a part for your car from a car shop. You had other tasks planned in the same area. When you get there, you find out they don't have that part in stock.

Now, you can do one of two things:

Go to the nearest auto shop to buy your car parts and see if you can do the other tasks in the new area you're in.

Or stay in that area, do other tasks you had already planned, and then go buy the car parts from the other shop.

Command

When you need something, you should know how to command answers and respect to get your job done. You should be in control.

Especially if you are supervising people, you must give good commands for them to do the job for you. Otherwise, you will not get your job done.

You must have discipline. If you are doing your job in the way that it needs to be done and completing it within the given time, that's discipline.

You are showing responsibility. Believe me—it catches on.

I was once the General Secretary of a non-profit organization. I had to call meetings and check the quorum. We were twelve people on the Executive Committee.

In the first meeting after I was elected, I was shocked to see members of the Executive Committee showing up late. Out of twelve, only two showed up on time. The other ten were five to forty-five minutes late.

I told them this would not work and that next time, if we did not have a quorum (seven) within fifteen minutes, there would be no meeting.

The next time, almost everybody started coming on time or within five minutes of the start time. That was a great achievement, given the mentality of that group.

But to achieve this, I had to show them that I was punctual myself. If I had been undisciplined and late, how would I be able to lay down the law?

<u>Organization Part 1</u>

Home – At home, everything should be in its place. Have a set time for everything.

If you must do a certain thing every day, then set aside a time (one hour or so) in the evening and let everyone know that you will not be available and cannot be disturbed during that time.

<u>Organization Part 2</u>

If you don't need it, then file it or throw it away. *(Add a table of what to keep and for how long.)*

If you have not used it in a year, and it does not have sentimental value, then it can be thrown away.

Write down what you do every day.

When do you get up?

When do you eat?

What do you eat?

How do you go to work?

What do you do there?

When do you come back?

What route do you take?

What do you do after coming back?

This will not be any good if you do not review it within a day or two. You should find ways to improve your lifestyle—to improve your quality of life.

You will notice:

Things you should continue doing

Things you should stop doing

Things you probably need to change a little

Change either in timing or with a minor adjustment. For example:

If you are eating late, maybe you need to eat dinner a little earlier.

If you watch a lot of TV, then you probably need to do that a little less.

Teamwork

Teamwork means the cooperative effort of a team. Team members in your group must push in the same direction.

For that to happen, goals must be clearly defined at team formation. Once the goals are established, everyone should agree on the course of action. Tasks should be divided in a way that leads to the agreed-upon goals.

One of the best ways to do this is to create a list of tasks for the team. This list should include:

The names of individuals doing each task

The expected date of completion

One person should drive the project to completion with accountability for all.

Synergy

Synergy is the interaction or cooperation of two or more organizations or groups.

When two organizations—or groups within an organization—are working together, there should be cooperation between them so that the project they are working on moves forward.

If synergy is missing, then things will fall apart, and the project will suffer.

You need to be on top of your part of the project. A list of things to do and a date of completion for each must be maintained to keep you on schedule.

If you have to lead the project, then keeping all groups working in harmony would be one of your main focuses. This is synergy.

Synergy starts with *yourself*, and then between the groups involved in the project. If the project involves other companies, then it becomes even more important to establish synergy as quickly as possible.

Delegation

When you must delegate, keep the following points in mind:

• Harmony

There should be chemistry between you and the person you are delegating to. I'm not saying you both should think alike, but the person should fully understand at a minimum:

What you want

How you want the work completed

When you want it done

• Information Sharing

Harmony can be achieved through proper communication. Provide all the necessary details to get the job completed efficiently.

• Competition/Governance Starts with You

There may be more than one person working on the same project—either in different sections or entirely different ones. A sense of competition can be healthy if it leads to better outcomes. But if it leads to jealousy, it becomes toxic. Your job is to keep an eye on your team and ensure only positive competition develops.

• Command

You are the person in authority, and this must be clear from the beginning. If it's not, confusion will arise. Clarify who is in charge, and give that person enough space to lead without stress.

• Say Thank You

Some people work for money, others volunteer. In either case, there's no excuse for being rude. If you are respectful, people will want to work with you again. Always say thank you after a job is done. When people see this behavior, they are more likely to treat others the same way and respect the culture you're creating.

• Trust

You must trust the person you're delegating to. If you can't rely on their work ethic or punctuality, the delegation will fail.

• Let Them Perform – Don't Micromanage

Let them do their job. This doesn't mean blind trust—just don't hover. Give them guidance, then step back. Periodically ask for updates, but allow some freedom.

• Invite and Value Feedback

Everyone has ideas. If someone suggests an improvement, don't take offense. If it improves efficiency, implement it and thank them for the input.

• Have Fun

Even serious work can be enjoyable. Keep in perspective what matters in life—God, family, and friends. Jobs and tasks come and go, but the people around you are what matter. Enjoy the work, and don't bring stress home.

• Take Others on Your Ride

If you're working on a high-profile task or business, bring along family or friends for the experience. Let them share in the journey.

• Optimists Only

Stay away from people with defeatist mentalities. Even if they're not mean-spirited, their negativity can drain your energy. Avoid assigning them new tasks or leadership roles.

• Turn Pessimists into Optimists

If you have the time and patience, you can try to guide them into a more positive outlook. If not, limit their influence in your space. Negative energy is contagious—so is positivity.

• Avoid Panic

If something unexpected happens, stop. Step back. Rework the list and change priorities. Don't jump into something unplanned without clear direction and objectives.

• Teamwork

Choose people who work well in team environments. One bad attitude can ruin team chemistry and jeopardize the entire project. If someone needs help, offer it—or assign others to support them. Motivate them using positive reinforcement. Predefine any rewards or consequences.

• Key Players

Identify and retain your top performers. Even if some tasks seem small, these are the people you can rely on. Train them if needed. Pay them above market value if you must, but keep them. They are your LeBron James, Michael Jordan, or Tom Brady. They will drive your success.

• Define Roles

When assigning tasks, define:

The scope of work

What completion looks like

Timeframes

Expectations and consequences if deadlines are missed

For teams, define each person's role clearly so there's no confusion.

• Compassion

Do not assign tasks to someone unprepared for them. You'll risk failure on both sides. If someone is struggling, help them. Train them quickly or reassign them to a more suitable role.

• Empathy

Life happens. If someone on your team has a personal emergency—illness, accident, family crisis—give them time off. Let others fill in temporarily. Reward the team once the project is completed. This will boost morale and loyalty.

Delegation Issues

Sometimes, it's okay to decide that a task just isn't worth delegating—either because the time, cost, or return doesn't justify it.

For example, you could spend hours in the sun combing a junkyard for old fencing wire and save a few dollars, or just buy new wire and save time. That time might be worth more to you.

Why Don't We Delegate?

We want control

We're afraid of losing it

We want to keep the power to ourselves

Why Should We Delegate?

You can't do everything at once

Delegation helps complete multiple tasks quickly

Others might know how to do it better

You can provide support either directly or by adding manpower

Use positive motivation. Have predetermined rewards or consequences.

Who Should We Delegate To?

Competent people

People you can trust

Intelligent, responsible individuals

What Should We Delegate?

Tasks that are beyond your skillset

Tasks that don't contain sensitive or confidential information

---

When Should We Delegate?

When you're too busy

When you're under a time crunch

When there are too many tasks

When others can do a better job

Stay in Command

Know what's done and what's pending. Don't micromanage, but stay aware. Be ready to solve problems or offer help when needed.

Have Fun

Enjoy your work. Enjoy your home life. Enjoy life in general.

If you're miserable doing a task, chances are you won't do it well.

So, have fun—even while doing the hard stuff.

CHAPTER 6

SETBACKS & SOLUTIONS

SETBACKS

Setbacks aren't just something that get in the way of making lists and accomplishing objectives; they're also things that will always be there. If you know how to cope with them, they can help you grow and get better. The most crucial part of successful list management is knowing how problems and answers are related. It turns possible failures into steps that lead to success.

Understanding the Nature of Setbacks

There are many ways that setbacks can arise in both our personal and work life. They happen when we can't do what we meant to do, even though we planned it meticulously. When hours go by faster than planned, it can cause problems with time, like not finishing activities and getting priorities mixed up. Another type of setback that comes from having limited resources is when the tools, people, or information needed to fulfill goals suddenly become unavailable or not enough.

Sometimes, the mental impacts of setbacks are harder to deal with than the physical ones. When people come into challenges they didn't expect, they typically experience a lot of bad things, like anger, grief, and even a sense of failure. But this normal emotional response might make it challenging to find good responses.

You shouldn't want to give up when you face setbacks; instead, you should want to keep going. Every difficulty we face teaches us something about how we plan, how well we can carry out those plans, and how we manage our resources. When we look at losses this way, they transition from being failures to chances to learn that will help us develop better lists and attain our goals in the future.

The key is to realize that problems are only temporary, not permanent. Things don't always go as planned, but that doesn't mean we can't be successful in the end. If you conceive at setbacks as challenges instead of failures, you will be better able to overcome difficulties.

The Form of Mistakes

Mistakes are what cause every setback, and knowing what these mistakes are is the first step in coming up with good answers. When you keep a list or try to attain a goal, you can make three basic sorts of blunders: scheduling mistakes, planning mistakes, and execution mistakes.

When we don't think about the natural rhythms and restrictions of our daily lives or when we guess wrong about how long specific tasks would take, we make scheduling mistakes. Some of these mistakes could be not realizing how hard a project is, not giving ourselves enough time between chores, or not thinking about things that could change our plans. A scheduling mistake could be as simple as thinking that a task that takes thirty minutes can be done in fifteen minutes, or as difficult as not taking into account how different projects depend on each other.

If we make mistakes when planning, it shows we didn't set our goals up well. Planning mistakes are like an architect neglecting to put a bedroom in the plans for a project. When we don't pay attention to crucial components of our goals or don't think about the resources and actions we need, these things happen. We usually make these mistakes because we didn't receive enough knowledge, didn't study enough, or didn't think about all the people and things that need to be done to attain our goals.

Execution mistakes occurs when the plan is in place but the work that needs to be done doesn't go as planned. These could be using the improper methods, not following the rules, or letting other vital duties and distractions get in the way of focused work. We often make mistakes because we don't know what we can accomplish and what we think we need to do.

The first step to rectifying a mistake is to realize that you made one. You can't fix things if you don't confess you made a mistake. We need to be honest with ourselves and be willing to look at how we do things objectively in order to earn this recognition. Not admitting mistakes at work might cause you to make the same ones over and over again, which can damage your relationships with coworkers and clients. In close relationships, faults that aren't acknowledged might lead to irritation and goals that aren't accomplished.

Once faults are found, they need to be examined more extensively to figure out what went wrong. Instead of focusing on individual problems, this inquiry should look at systemic issues. Did we make the mistake because we didn't have enough information, the correct tools, the right timing, or anything else that was beyond our control? If we know what created the problem, we can come up with particular solutions that repair the problem at its source instead of just treating the symptoms.

<u>Distinguishing between Problems and Challenges</u>
You need to grasp the difference between difficulties and obstacles in order to solve problems properly. Each one needs a distinct strategy and answer. Things that are out of our control and make it hard for us to move forward are called obstacles. Instead of tackling them head-on, they make us find a way around them. On the other hand, challenges are difficulties that we can overcome by being inventive, working hard, and planning ahead.

We could get into a traffic accident that keeps us from getting to an important meeting, our equipment could break down and stop work on a project, or we could get sick suddenly and not be able to stick to our schedule. You need to be able to adapt and find new ways to go about, procure backup equipment, or change your plans to match the new situation in these situations. We need to be adaptable and have backup plans that enable us move around challenges instead of getting stuck by them.

We can learn and grow when we face challenges and find new ways to tackle them. If a meeting is canceled, the next step is to find another way to get in touch with that person and finish the assignment. When a project has technical challenges, it might be challenging to find ways to fix them, learn new things, or put together the best team to get the job done. When we face problems, we have to grow and find new approaches to attain our goals.

The way you look at things and how ready you are can often make the difference between a problem and a challenge. If someone didn't check the weather and brought an umbrella, they might have a terrible time with a sudden rainstorm. If they did check the weather and came prepared, they would only have a tiny problem. For instance, if someone doesn't know how to fix a computer problem, it could be a major deal for them. But if they do know how to fix it or can get help from someone who does, it might not be such a big deal.

If you plan, you can reduce potential issues into manageable obstacles. We may minimize the possibility that something unexpected will completely stop us by thinking ahead about what could go wrong and creating arrangements for how to deal with it. Being ready could mean finding additional suppliers, having extra equipment on hand, or making friends with people who can support you when you need it.

Let's Look at How We Can Find Solutions

The list below will help you understand the situation and then figure out what to do and how to do it.

Overcoming Setbacks: Obstacles, Challenges, and Mistakes

1. Obstacles
2. Challenges – Find Solutions
3. Mistakes – Learn From Them
4. Work Smarter
5. Pick Your Battles (Tasks)
6. Make Your Mission Possible (It's Not Impossible)
7. Find Solutions (Look for Them)
8. Avoid Panic

1. **Obstacles**

Obstacles are not challenges; they are roadblocks.

They stop you cold.

Think of it like this: you're driving to an appointment, and there's been a major accident. The road is blocked. You can't remove the accident—you have to wait, reroute, or take a detour.

These are obstacles.

- You can't always control them, but you can control your response:
- Wait it out
- Change your route
- Use traffic apps and plan ahead

Life obstacles can look like:

Your car won't start before an important errand

Someone calls you with an urgent, unexpected issue

You're headed out and suddenly get a flat tire

Adapt. Reschedule. Find alternate paths.

---

2. **Challenges**

Challenges are tough tasks, but not roadblocks.

They test your creativity, stamina, and problem-solving skills.

Example:

You're going on a scheduled trip to Houston, but the person you're meeting cancels last minute. Instead of canceling your trip, offer alternatives:

"Can we meet later in the evening?"

"Can we reschedule for tomorrow or the day after?"

Give options, show commitment, and you'll likely still get the meeting—and respect.

I tell my children

Don't just complain—solve

Once you solve it, you're welcome to complain, if it helps—but not before.

Think of challenges as navigation:

You're at point A and want to get to point B

You know traffic is bad in some areas

You plan your route based on the map—not just GPS, but your strategy

There are many ways to solve one problem. Below are many ways to get to 12. Similarly, if one solution doesn't work, then go to the next option or next, or next.

$6 + 6 = 12$

$1 \times 12 = 12$

$2 \times 6 = 12$

$3 \times 4 = 12$

$4 \times 3 = 12$

$6 \times 2 = 12$

$12 \times 1 = 12$

Pick the solution that suits your current situation best. Tomorrow, the right answer might be different. That's okay.

Even in sports, football teams switch tactics when their standard game plan fails. They run trick plays. Maybe they don't always work, but they throw off the defense and make room for future success.

3. **Mistakes**

People often point out others' mistakes but rarely own up to their own.

That creates tension—in teams, in relationships, in families. If you don't own your mistakes, you're not growing. You're not improving. You're choosing to stay the same or get worse.

Growth comes from reflection.

Set aside time—maybe 15 minutes a day. Sit down and ask yourself:

What did I do right today?

What mistakes did I make?

What can I do differently tomorrow?

This isn't just about your career—this is about your entire life.

Maybe:

You didn't have the tools

You weren't trained

You lacked the information

You didn't care enough

Whatever the reason, acknowledge it.

Solutions:

Ask for help

Seek advice from friends, family, or professionals

Take courses

Train yourself

Invest in the right tools

Build a team to support you

If you can't do a job, don't fake it—find someone who can.

This is not weakness—this is wisdom.

When someone points out your mistake, thank them (unless their intention is harmful—be wise). Most people are trying to help you grow.

If someone makes a mistake, don't jump to blame. Instead, ask:

Was it a scheduling mistake?

A planning mistake?

An execution mistake?

Find it. Fix it. Learn from it. Then don't repeat it. Mistakes aren't always about doing something *wrong*. Sometimes they're about not doing what was needed—missing a deadline, failing to plan, or not acting when required.

For example:

If you don't plan your house with a patio, you won't have one. That's not a construction mistake—it's a planning oversight. Planning mistakes often come back to bite us—just like relationship mistakes. If you make one, own it, fix it, apologize, and move forward.

Especially in business:

If you deliver one project late, the customer may forgive you. Deliver late, and you'll likely lose them.

Remember This About Mistakes:

a) Own your mistake.

b) Get training or tools if needed.

c) Don't repeat it.

d) If needed, delegate to someone more capable.

4. **Work Smarter**

It means knowing what you are doing and what is the best way to get where you want to go. Know what has not worked previously and what has not worked in your case. Find the best solution for you—that is working smarter. It means not scheduling things you know you cannot do that day or will not do a good job on. If you put it on the list and it will take multiple hours, it may keep you from working on other, more important and urgent tasks. You must move it to the future, not today. Working smarter means working accurately, faster, and with dedication. It means having things ready even before you initiate a task. Have the necessary workforce ready before you start a task. Have your tools ready, have manpower ready, and have enough time to finish that task.

5. **Pick Your Battles**

We just talked about taking on doable tasks. Some tasks will require a longer time than others. If they hinder tasks that require immediate attention, then move them to the future if possible, or create extra time so you can get that task done. Sometimes it will take three hours to complete a particular task, but you also have other tasks that need to be done. You have a time crunch. You must start early so you can complete all tasks on the same day. If you must start early, then start early. If you must end late, then end late. You must do what you must do. There is no way around it. You must move other tasks around or, as we have talked about, outsource. Ask your family or friends to help out. You do this because the task needs to be done and it cannot be moved forward.

To create time, don't watch TV, take some time off your lunch or dinner, or reschedule your social assignment if you have any excuse, if possible. If the task is not related to work, then take a day off and complete the task. If it is work-related, then go to work early or stay late.

---

6. **Mission Possible**

(It's Not Impossible)

If it is related to work and looks impossible, then go to your boss and discuss it with him/her. Let your boss know that the project requires more time or headcount. Discuss with your boss ways to handle the task in the most efficient way possible.

Break it down into ten-minute intervals. Don't take any phone calls. That way, you can concentrate on what you are doing. If somebody visits your cube, then tell that person you are busy and will be back with him/her shortly or as soon as your task is done.

Nothing is impossible.

You have heard this many times. Nothing is impossible. I read somewhere that if somebody tells you "Nothing is impossible," ask them to put skis horizontally on their shoulders and go through a revolving door. Fun aside, there are a few things that are impossible not because they cannot be done, but because good training, tools, or enough good people are not provided to get the job done. If the task is taking too much of your time and you still cannot do it even after outsourcing it, then you need to go back to the drawing board to see what can be done to resolve the issue. If you cannot handle a business, then maybe the best thing to do is to sell the business and do something you can handle.

There is always a solution. Don't take tasks that you cannot do, and then think it is impossible. It's too late now. You should have trained yourself or hired help to do the tasks successfully. You cannot build a house yourself. You can, if you know how to, but if you don't have the training or resources, then don't even attempt it. That is the case with a lot of tasks that you might come up against that you are not trained to do. Another example is fixing a car. If you are not trained, then you cannot fix it. It's that simple.

Don't make a task impossible for yourself. Impossible means you cannot do it yourself, or you cannot outsource it once you have started. It's better to recognize this before you start on a task and hire somebody to do it.

---

7. **Find Solutions**

This is one of the most important life lessons: *find solutions*. I've told my children this over and over again. Problems happen every day, but each one comes with a solution. Find it.

Some people react to problems by whining or blaming others. That's because they don't know the solution or they're avoiding responsibility. Don't be like that.

Who? Why? How?

In critical situations, find the solution first. You can figure out the who and why later.

In non-urgent situations, investigate. Who caused the issue? How did it happen? Not to place blame—but to understand. Maybe it was a lack of training. Maybe someone's overworked or burned out. Maybe they didn't have the right tools. Maybe the process itself is flawed.

Understanding what went wrong is how you avoid repeating it. Sometimes it is someone's fault—especially if they're negligent or repeat offenders. In that case, you may need to remove them from the position.

When time is limited:

Find a solution.

What caused the problem?

Who caused the problem?

When there's time:

What caused the problem?

Who caused the problem?

Find a solution.

There might be more than one solution. Go with the one that has more pros than cons.

---

8. **<u>Avoid Panic</u>**

This is the worst thing you can do. If things are getting too hectic and you feel like you're losing control, the best thing to do in these conditions is to stop doing everything and take a little break. Panic leads to bad decision-making and poor execution. Relax—this is not the end of the world. There is still life to live outside this task or job. You cannot add stress to your life. It will only ruin your health. Stress leads to many diseases—heart attacks and high blood pressure are two of them. So, step back, relax, close your eyes, and take a break in a quiet, secluded area. Take deep breaths. Think of ways to solve your issues.

If something happened that you had not planned for, then redo the list and redo the priorities. Stop and step back to think and plan. Nothing is worse than going into something you haven't planned for and not knowing your direction or objectives. I used to watch Bear Grylls' *Man vs. Wild*. He would always say to find out which direction you need to go. Find your direction—and then move.

A lot of people panic in a crowd. Avoid panic. If you have been asked to make a decision with other people around and you haven't made up your mind yet, take a step back and relax. Review your situation, come to an informed conclusion, and then decide. If you do this, the probability is that your decision will be wise—and even if it takes extra time, others will appreciate it.

You hear gunshots—the first thing you should do is fall to the ground. If you have family with you, then you cannot afford to panic. Make sure they also do the same. You must take care of them as well.

Avoid panic at work. By panicking, you will not complete any of your tasks. Again—relax, close your eyes, or do whatever helps you unwind. Make a list. Take the shortest or easiest task, complete it, and move on to the next one. You will feel better, your confidence will go up, and your stress level will go down. The next task should also be the shortest or easiest one, if possible. If you must do a task that is hard but due "yesterday," then break it down into a manageable load and dive into it without any distractions.

Sometimes, when you see a lot of tasks in front of you, you panic. Clear your desk and take on one task at a time. Move the bigger task to later.

Do Not Get Angry – Make Sure Mistakes Do Not Happen Again

Anger rarely helps—whether it's at work, home, in business, or with family. Yes, there are situations where you have good reason to be angry, such as when someone is abusing you. But generally, it's best to maintain your composure.

Respect is reciprocated when you show it. People will respect you, even if they don't like you at first. They might eventually come to like you as well. Perhaps you didn't adequately explain why someone didn't perform up to par. Examine yourself, too.

Maybe they don't have enough manpower or tools. I've seen teams overburdened with work and using software that didn't function properly. Frustration increases when quality declines. Imagine yourself in their position. Be fair. Strive to help others reach their potential, but don't go overboard. Speak up if your circumstances are unfair. Even if management is unable to resolve the issue, provide solutions. Make an effort to ease the stress.

You can't hold it against your child if they can't change a flat tire correctly or if they're doing it too slowly if you haven't taught them how to do it. To expect positive outcomes, you must first train them. Effective training is essential. If someone is giving it their all and still having trouble, there may be a problem with the training or the workload, or perhaps they are in a situation that doesn't allow them to perform to their maximum potential. Don't lose your temper. You have to assist the person in getting superior outcomes. Look for a different job that better fits their temperament, personality, education, or all three.

One Last Thing About Training

During training, take notes on everything and follow instructions to the letter. Some people are poor educators, and they may later say something different from what they stated at first—and attempt to hold you accountable for a "mistake." You can get yourself out of a difficult situation if you have decent notes.

CHAPTER 7

CLEANUP & COMPLETION

Work Never Ends

This isn't the end. It never stops, for better or for worse. Thank goodness, because what would you do if you didn't have anything to do? Life would get dull. Things will keep arriving at you, both good and bad, and you'll have to deal with them for the rest of your life.

There is always work to do. There is always something happening in your business, personal, or social life. You will always have something to do. You need to find a way to deal with it. You will succeed if you face it with heart and a plan. If you don't, the work will consume your life. You won't have time for yourself or your family. You won't even have time to do your job.

At first, this truth might seem too much to handle. The never-ending list of duties, commitments, and chances can feel like a heavy load on your shoulders. However, you can also view it this way. Life has a rhythm and a purpose because there are always new tasks and problems to solve. Without them, days would run together and have no meaning or purpose.

When you have nothing to do, think of your retirement or vacation. At first, the freedom feels great. You may sleep in, watch TV, or just relax without having to worry about anything. But after a few days or weeks, something fantastic happens. You begin to feel antsy. You start to look for things to do, projects to work on, or issues to solve. It's not a weakness in your character that you feel restless; it's just how people are. We are meant to be active, helpful, and involved in the world around us.

You can't and shouldn't get rid of work from your life. The most important thing is to handle it well so that it helps you instead of hurting you. If you have the correct attitude and tools, work may be a source of happiness and success instead of stress and overwhelm.

Your lists are the main way you keep track of this never-ending flow. They help you keep track of everything that needs your attention, put it in a form that makes sense, and deal with it in a planned method. Without lists, work that never ends can get out of hand and become too much to handle. It becomes organized and possible using lists.

The key is to understand that you will never get to a point where everything is done. There will always be another email to respond to, another project to begin, another friendship to build, and another skill to learn. If you accept this fact, you can stop trying to reach the unachievable goal of finishing and start working toward the more realistic aim of making progress.

End of the Day

At the end of the day, you should go back and see what you accomplished all day, not just the things you had to do but also the things you did that weren't on your to-do list. You should have marked off the tasks you finished and left the remainder open. How many things did you get done? Is there still something on your plate that you were expected to do but didn't—or couldn't—finish?

You probably still have something. You should check the list you made last night or this morning to see how much of the job is done and how much is left.

This daily evaluation is more than just keeping track of money. It's a time to think about your habits, how much work you can get done, and how much you can handle. You will be shocked at how much you did on certain days. Some days you'll be confused about where the time went. Both of these things are normal and useful.

Take a minute to think about what you accomplished as you look at the items you marked off. Every item that is done shows effort, focus, and follow-through. These are not little things. The ability to start and finish things is a big deal in a society full of distractions and conflicting demands.

Don't be too hard on yourself for the things you still need to do. Instead, try to figure out what happened. Did the job take longer than you thought it would? Did something important come up that stopped you? Did you find out that the job was harder than you first thought? Was your energy level different from what you anticipated? Knowing these things will help you make better plans in the future.

You should also think about what you did when you weren't working. Family and friends are just as vital as tasks. Did you chat to your spouse or kids? Were you able to talk to your mom and dad? Were you kind to others? Did you help someone you didn't know? Did you say something mean or become mad at someone? These are crucial. Being nice to others can help you stay calm and happy, which will help you deal with your daily problems more quickly and easily.

This wider look at life recognizes that it is about more than just getting things done. Your relationships, your character, and how you affect other people are equally as important as the work you do, if not more so. In the truest sense, a day spent getting a lot done while being unpleasant to coworkers or frustrated with your family is not a good day.

Take note of the times when you're not doing anything. When someone talked to you, did you listen? Did you see something nice in your surroundings? Did you say thank you or show your appreciation? These times are often more important to your day than the number of things you checked off your list.

The end-of-day review also includes recognizing the good things that happened that you didn't expect. You might have had an intriguing talk with a coworker, gotten wonderful news, or just had a really good lunch. These unanticipated good things are typically the best parts of our days, but we sometimes forget about them because we're so focused on getting things done.

Reward Yourself

You should give yourself a prize for what you did. If you finished something major or big on your list, reward yourself. There is time for fun as well as work. You need to establish some limits. You should reward yourself if you accomplish something on time or do a good job on a task. Eat out or see a movie. You might also wait until the end of the week to get the reward and make it greater. You might set a goal of 100 tasks and then reward yourself with something large.

Industrious people often forget about the idea of self-reward. People often go on to the next work right away without taking a moment to appreciate what they just did. This method misses a great chance to encourage good conduct and keep people motivated over time.

You don't have to spend a lot of money or make things complicated to reward someone. A cup of your favorite coffee, a brief walk outside, a few minutes reading something you like, or a phone call to someone you care about are all simple pleasures that may be quite rewarding. The most important thing is that the reward feels fair for what you did and is something you appreciate.

You shouldn't put off your reward for so long that you cease to like your work. You should reward yourself with minor things as well as big ones. One of the most important things is to be happy. The best thing you can give yourself is happiness; it's worth more than money or things. Things and money come and go. Money and things will never be as satisfying as they seem if you're not happy.

This view of happiness as the highest reward changes the way we think about productivity. You're not trying to get outside approval or collect things; instead, you're trying to reach a condition of being that improves every part of your life. Happy people are more creative, stronger, kinder, and better at practically everything they do.

Yes, you might feel sad at times. But if you have a joyful soul, you will be happy no matter how much money you spend. A flower, a sunrise or sunset, a gentle breeze, a sunny day in winter, or rain in summer can all provide a different level of peace and joy. Most of the time, these things are free. Someone who has a positive attitude will be happy no matter where they are. Someone who thinks negatively will always be unhappy.

This insight about discovering joy in simplicity is profound. It implies that happiness is more about how you see things than about your situation. You can make every day more joyful by training yourself to notice and enjoy the little things. This doesn't mean pretending that everything is OK or disregarding concerns. It involves learning how to discover the good in bad situations.

When you reward yourself, you also learn an essential lesson about taking care of yourself. People are often very nice to others but not very nice to themselves. Recognizing your own hard work and being kind to yourself is a good way to build a strong base for long-term health and productivity.

Evaluate Yourself

Every night before you go to bed, think about the work you did that day and then think about yourself. Look for ways to make your work better and yourself better. How many of the things on the list have you done? What would it take to get the ones that aren't done done?

This nightly review has several uses. First, it helps you end the day and switch your thinking from work mode to rest mode. Second, it makes you conscious of your habits and patterns, which is the first step in making things better. Third, it lets you learn from both your achievements and your mistakes, which makes you better over time.

The evaluation should be fair but not too harsh. You're seeking for facts, not excuses to beat yourself up. Ask something like, "What went well today?" What was harder than you thought it would be? What would I do differently? What did I find out? These questions help you learn important things from what you do every day.

You should also make a list for the next day so that when you go to bed, you already know what you need to do. We talked about spending five minutes in the morning going over the list of things we had to do that day. You may think of it as getting ready the night before and then getting a reminder the next morning.

There are several benefits to making a list for tomorrow the night before. While you sleep, it helps your subconscious mind think about the things you need to do. This can sometimes lead to new ideas or answers by morning. It also helps you avoid decision fatigue the next day because you wake up knowing what you need to do instead of having to figure it out while you're tired.

You might also forget to make the list, or something can come up before bed that makes it hard for you to do it. If you set aside some time for yourself in the morning, you can make the list then. You might want to change the order of the items on the list based on new information that has come up after you made it. On the other hand, if you can't find five minutes in the morning for any reason and you made the list the night before, you're ahead of schedule and won't miss a beat. You could even have to add some additional things to do.

This flexibility in time shows that life doesn't always go according to plan. Having a system that works no matter when you plan is the most crucial thing.

It doesn't matter if you plan at night or in the morning; the important thing is to always plan on purpose.

You should also think about how you've grown as a person during the review process. Are you getting more patient? More put together? More focused? Are you learning skills that are important to you? Are you making a positive difference in the lives of others? These questions assist make sure that your work is more than just getting things done.

Solutions

You might not have been able to do some things or they might not have worked out. You need to discover solutions in those situations. What do you need to do to finish the jobs you haven't finished yet? You might need to change what you're doing or give yourself extra time to finish the assignment.

Finding solutions is where genuine learning takes place. There is always a reason why projects are not finished or don't work. Sometimes the reason is outside of the person's control, including an unexpected interruption, a change in circumstances, or new information that changes the task. Sometimes the issue is internal, such as not knowing how long something will take, not having the right talents, or not being motivated enough.

External factors typically need real-world answers. If you were often interrupted, you might need to find a calmer place to work or make your limits clearer. You could have to tweak the assignment or get rid of it altogether if things change. If you found out something new, you might need to do more research or talk to other people.

Different kinds of solutions are needed for internal problems. You might need to keep better track of your time if you always underestimate how long things will take. You may need to pay for training or ask for support if you don't have the abilities you require. You might need to remember why you are doing the activity or break it down into smaller, easier-to-manage parts if you aren't feeling motivated.

Do you need to buy something to assist you finish the job? Put that on your calendar now. If you need to change your car's headlight but don't have the right tools, add "buy tools" to your list. That is figuring out a way to fix it.

This example shows a crucial point: solutions typically require more work. Instead of seeing this as a problem, use it as a chance to be clear. When you figure out what you need to do to finish a task, you turn a nebulous problem into a clear plan of action. When you need to change a headlight, you have to do two things: buy the tools you need and then change the headlight. This level of detail makes development possible.

Sometimes the best way to solve a problem is to completely change how you do things. If you keep trying to do a task and it never gets done, it could be the wrong task or the incorrect way to do it. There might be an easier way to get the same outcome, or maybe the assignment isn't as critical as you first believed.

The process of finding a solution also helps you improve your problem-solving skills in other areas outside managing tasks. Being able to look at problems, figure out what caused them, and come up with specific solutions is useful in all areas of life. You get better at dealing with problems the more you work through them.

The idea of making progress all the time

You will never finish your work. Things will constantly keep arriving. You only need to find the time and do it right away. That is the end of the cleanup and the duties that need to be done. There will always be more jobs to do. Completion is a misnomer. There can never be perfect completeness, but you can feel good about finishing things as they come and always moving on in life.

It is freeing to change your mind from wanting to finish things to wanting to keep making progress. It takes away the pressure to go to some imaginary place where everything is done and lets you enjoy the process itself. Every task you finish is a win, not because it gets you closer to your goal, but because it shows that you are making progress, putting in effort, and being able to do things.

In this case, "cleanup and completion" doesn't mean ending everything for good. This entails going through what's in front of you on a regular basis, deciding what's most important, and then doing something about those things. It's a never-ending cycle of checking, doing, and changing.

A lot of people would be bored if there was nothing to do. You need to find things that make you happy, do things that make you happy, and do things that make you happy. Happiness is not just for you; it's also for your family, friends, relatives, and everyone else you know.

Instead of seeing labor as a burden, this view sees it as an opportunity. There are always chances to grow, help, and be happy since there are always tasks and difficulties to do. The most important thing is to pick projects and ways of doing things that are in line with your values and help you and others feel good.

Your happiness has a ripple effect that goes beyond you. You make the world a better place for everyone around you when you do your work with a good attitude and enjoy it. Your family benefits from your happiness, your coworkers benefit from your positive energy, and your community benefits from what you do.

Because everything is connected, working hard and being happy are not selfish goals. They help everyone whose life you touch in a good way. You may help people, be present in relationships, and support causes that matter to you when you do your work well and keep a happy attitude.

This question is both simple and deep. The answer is usually straightforward because it has to do with basic human needs and wants, including having meaningful connections, doing work that matters, growing as a person, and being part of something bigger than oneself. It's deep because to really answer it, you have to think deeply about yourself and have the fortitude to make sure that what you do every day matches your own ideals.

When it comes to lists and getting things done, this question helps you decide what to do. When you have a lot to do or a lot of things to pick from, asking yourself "What makes me happy?" might help you choose activities that not only need to be done but also make you feel better and happier in general.

Being happy at work doesn't entail merely doing what you like right now. Happiness can come from doing hard tasks that help you reach your long-term goals. Sometimes it comes from helping others, even when it's not easy. Sometimes it comes from doing hard work that teaches you discipline and skills.

The question changes throughout time as well. What makes you happy at one stage of life could be different from what makes you happy at another level. If you think about this issue often, it will help you keep your lists and priorities in line with your present values and situation instead of old ideas about what should matter to you.

The best thing about lists is that they may help you live with purpose, not merely get things done. Your lists become instruments for making a meaningful life instead of merely a productive one when they reflect your beliefs, promote your health, and add to your happiness and the happiness of others.

So, the cleanup and completion phase is truly about closing the gap between what you want to do and what you do. It's also about finishing the work of being the person you want to be while making the world a better place. It's never done, and that's how it should be.

So, the question comes back to you:

What makes you happy?

ABOUT THE AUTHOR

Syed Akbar is a fervent supporter of order, simplicity, and meaningful living. He has spent years researching how lists may change the way we think, plan, and behave, with a keen focus on useful tools that make life easier. According to Syed, lists are a way of thinking, a technique, and a mirror reflecting what really matters—they are more than just reminders. He wrote this book to provide readers the tools they need to take charge of their time, energy, and objectives by drawing on his own experience, careful observation, and dedication to helping others succeed.

Syed demonstrates how the modest list can be an effective tool for clarity and advancement, whether it is for focusing through life's stress or breaking down enormous aspirations into manageable steps. His conviction that anyone can live more consciously is reflected in this book, and it all begins with making a plan and seeing it through to completion.

www.ingramcontent.com/pod-product-compliance
Lightning Source LLC
Chambersburg PA
CBHW051442130726
47987CB00005B/2153